LIFE UPON
the wicked stage

JOAN CAMPBELL
with Pamela Cockerill

"Wild old men who give you jewels and sables
Only live in Aesop's Fables.
Life upon the wicked stage
Ain't nothin' for a girl."

Jerome Kern

CONTENTS

INTRODUCTION

By the early sixties, most people had a television in their home, and live theatre was facing hard times. Stage musicals like Lilac Time, which had given me a living for nearly fifteen years, were beginning to be seen as rather old-fashioned, so work was becoming very hard to find for professional singers like me.

To keep the wolf from the door I had started doing cabaret acts in the working men's clubs of Yorkshire. These clubs were always crowded and often got quite rowdy as the night wore on. The audience was kept in order by a chairman who used to thump his gavel before every act and say 'Nah then, Let's 'ave a bit oh 'ush for t'turn'

At that time there was a TV variety programme called The Wheeltappers and Shunters, with comedians and singers, which was based on a working men's club format, and it had helped make them very popular in the North of England. There were some good acts touring the clubs - in 1962, the singer Jackie Trent and the comedian Norman Collier were both doing the same circuit as me. The pay was very good. I usually only worked three or four nights a week, but I was paid more for those four nights than I'd been paid for a whole week singing light opera.

This was well before women's lib came along and female cabaret singers were expected to dress in a leotard and fishnet tights to keep the punters happy. Fortunately, I had good legs in those days which meant I was never short of someone to buy me a drink after the show!

One night I was performing at one of these Yorkshire clubs -I forget which one -when two smartly dressed men came up to me at the bar after I'd finished my act and started chatting. One of them was obviously quite taken with my outfit and seemed keen to get to know me better. He was tall, but apart from that, rather an ordinary looking man, with a strong West Riding accent. However, he was definitely out to impress me. He told me that his name was Fred and that he owned a large garage in Sheffield.

'I loved your act, love' he said. 'Where are you appearing next?'

'I'm off to Doncaster tomorrow night' I told him.

'Oh, I'll send a car to drive you to work. What time do you have to be there?'

The next day to my amazement, a huge flashy American Ford Fairlane convertible with the hood down, turned up at my digs. The driver told me he worked for Fred, and I was taken in style to the club where I was performing that night.

Later in the evening, Fred himself turned up at the club to watch my act. Afterwards he shadowed me to the bar, where he bought me an Americano cocktail (my favourite drink at the time) and carried on chatting me up where he'd left off the night before.

I had nearly finished my drink and was getting ready to leave when he said to me 'I've got an aeroplane- and I'd planned to fly to Le Touquet next weekend. Would you come with me?'

I was a bit taken aback and quite impressed. I'd never met anyone with his own aeroplane before. I wasn't sure whether to believe him or not, but I was always a bit of a daredevil and up for an adventure, so with barely a second thought I said okay.

Very early the following Thursday morning, he picked me up in the same flashy car and his man drove us out into the countryside and dropped us off in a grass field near Worksop where there was a small hangar. Fred opened up the hangar doors and revealed a tiny two seater single engine plane inside. I wasn't normally lost for words, but I'm sure my jaw actually dropped. I think I'd been imagining some sort of executive jet. The size of the flimsy machine that was expected to take us across the channel took me aback, to say the least.

However, the Fairline and its driver had already disappeared, so it looked as if I was committed. Nervously I followed Fred into the hangar.

'What can I do with my music?' I asked. I was booked to perform in Doncaster again the following night and I hadn't wanted to risk not having time to pick my music up from my digs so I'd brought it with me.

Fred opened a little cubby hole at the back of the plane, put my music and my overnight bag in there and screwed it down again. Then he got into the front and I had to clamber ungracefully into the seat behind him. In front of me, to my alarm, I found I had a set of controls. 'What am I supposed to do with these?' I asked.

Fred laughed 'Nothing. Whatever you do, don't touch them. Keep your legs wide apart and don't put your hands on that stick in the middle or you'll be steering the plane'.

I didn't need telling twice.

A few minutes later we were accelerating down the grass strip and our journey to France had begun. The flight seemed to last for ever, but eventually we found ourselves over the sea and a short time later I saw the French coast coming up. As we flew over the land, Fred started peering down, first to the left and then to the right. It gradually became obvious to me that he hadn't a clue where he was.

'Are we nearly at le Touquet?' I asked.

'No', he said sounding a bit cross, as he continued looking around him.

We were quite low by now and I could see brown corrugated fields underneath us with people working in them. The next thing I knew, the plane descended even further and I realised with a shock that we were going to land in the middle of this field.

How we didn't turn over I have no idea, but somehow we didn't and the plane just went bumpety bump for ages until, finally, it came to a rest. I looked across the field and saw a couple of farmworkers looking at us in amazement.

Fred had seen them too.

'Le Touquet?' he shouted across to them.

One of the men pointed. and from what I understood from my schoolgirl French, said 'Follow the river. Turn right'. I translated for Fred, as it was obvious he didn't understand a word. A moment later the engine roared and we took off, bumpety-bump again.

Once we were back up in the sky, we soon saw the river and by following it we finally landed at Le Touquet airport where he went in with our documents. We had to show our passports and various other papers. If anyone had reported our illegal landing earlier, I'm sure we'd been arrested on the spot, but luckily, nobody had. Once we were cleared by customs, we were able to get a taxi into the town. There, we found a little inn and booked two rooms.

It was a glorious day and only early afternoon. "Let's go down and enjoy the sea" Fred suggested, so we went to the beach, hired a couple of deckchairs and lay back to sunbathe. It was really hot and after a few minutes, he sat up and took off his shirt.

That was when I got another shock. Fred had obviously very recently had serious surgery. A long vivid red scar stretched all the way down his back from top to bottom.

'My goodness what's happened to you?' I asked.

'Oh, I've just had a lung removed' he said casually.

I was horrified. He was quite tall, but with his shirt off he was so thin and pale he looked as if a puff of wind would have blown him over. He was obviously a very poorly man and I'd had no idea. To be honest he didn't look to me as if he was in any state to drive a car, never mind a plane. I had already been worrying about the journey back. Now I felt even more nervous!

After the beach we had a nice dinner, then went to a bar for a few drinks and afterwards we retired very properly to our separate rooms. As I got ready for bed I thought again about his terrible scar and it occurred to me that maybe inviting me on this trip had been a defiant response to his illness, a final fling before he popped his clogs. If that was the reason, it was only a token gesture, because to my relief, not once during the trip had he had made any attempt to seduce me. Even so, I did lock my bedroom door that night!

The plan had always been to stay just the one night as Fred had to get back to work at his garage in Sheffield and I had to sing again the following evening at the Doncaster club. So the next morning, straight after breakfast, we set off back to the airport. This time we took off properly from tarmac and of course once we'd crossed the channel and were flying over England, Fred knew exactly where we were.

After a few hours we landed back on the little field with the hangar. Fred put the plane away and locked up the doors and we walked outside to wait for his chauffeur to collect us. Outside the hangar was a little hut which had a toilet in it. We were standing outside this hut when a car appeared in the distance coming down the track to the field. I guessed it was his driver come to pick us up and was about to set off to walk towards it when I realised it wasn't the Fairline, but a different car. Behind me I heard Fred say 'Oh my God'. I turned to look at him. He was as white as a sheet.

'My wife's come to fetch me' he said.

He grabbed my arm 'Quick, get in there' and he pushed me into the toilet and slammed the door shut. I hid behind the door, not daring to say a word as the sound of the car engine got louder and louder. It was the first time I had heard any mention of a wife. When I peeped out, I saw Fred scuttling towards the car. Then, to my horror he jumped in, the car turned around and away they went.

So there I was, in a field somewhere near Worksop, with all my music, which I needed for that night, still locked in the aeroplane. There was nothing for it but to set off walking. Eventually I reached the road and luckily for me, after a mile or so I came to a bus stop. I have no idea how long I waited there before a bus came along, but finally, after a couple of changes, and with a few hours to spare before I was due to start my act, I got myself to my digs in Doncaster.

But I still didn't have my music. What on earth was I going to do about it? Luckily Fred had told me the name of his garage. I looked it up in the phone book and rang the number and without giving my name, asked to be put through to him.

'Hello, who's this?' Fred's voice asked.

I decided to let him work that out for himself.

'Well, that was very nice' I said. 'Leaving me stuck in a field in Worksop. How am I going to perform tonight with all my music locked in the aeroplane?'

'Oh, it's you', he said, sounding irritated. Lowering his voice, he added 'I'm sorry Joan, but I can't do anything about that now, I'm very busy'.

I rarely swore, but on this occasion I made an exception.

'Well. You'd better bloody well do something about it, Fred' I said. 'Because if you don't, I shall arrive at your place and demand to see your wife. And then I'll tell her that you took me to Le Touquet. She won't know that nothing happened between us will she?'

There was a long silence at the other end of the line while he thought about it. Finally, he said grumpily 'All right. I'll send a man to pick you up.'

So he sent the same poor man as before to get the music from the hangar and then to pick me up from my digs and take me to the Working Men's Club where I was singing. Up until then I'd been ferried about like a film star in this big fancy Fairline. This time Fred's man was driving the biggest broken-down old banger you've ever seen!

I couldn't help laughing.

'This is a bit of a comedown' I said. 'Do you think this thing will get us to the club?'

The driver shook his head and grinned. Obviously he knew the score.

Somehow the car spluttered along and we arrived at the club with minutes to spare, so the day was saved.

I had no idea when I said yes, how it would all end up. I was stupid I suppose. After fifteen years in show business, perhaps I should have known better. But that was me. From the day I was born, I was always a bit of a daredevil, and as Katherine Hepburn once said - if you obey all the rules you miss all the fun!

CHAPTER 1

On the day I was born, I'm sure neither of my parents dreamed that their new daughter's future lay in show business. And they certainly couldn't have foreseen the sort of adventures it would lead me into.

I arrived in the world on September 18th 1930 in a bedroom above my father's butcher's shop on the marketplace in Hyde, near Manchester. It was a difficult birth. I had the cord around my neck and when I came out I was completely blue and not breathing. Luckily for me, my grandmother had been acting as an unofficial midwife to her neighbours for years and she came to the rescue. After she'd popped a few drops of brandy in my mouth, I coughed and choked and that was it. Nine months after they were married my parents had an extra mouth to feed.

My father's name was Harold Booth and his family had been butchers for generations. Booth's had a big shop with a slaughterhouse attached, where they used to kill their own cattle. If I'd been a boy I might have grown up to be a butcher, but luckily for me, my parents never pushed me in that direction. Another stroke of luck as far as my future was concerned was that my father was musical. He played the piano very well and as a boy he had sung in the local choir, so whenever the radio was turned on in our house it was generally tuned to music.

Another of Father's talents was swimming and he used to play for Hyde's water polo team, Hyde Seal which was quite famous. Father was a short man, but very strong. He used to do a trick to amuse me and my sisters of emptying a box of matches and putting the outer pack on the floor. Then he'd do a handstand, lower his face and pick up the matchbox with his nose. All that swimming and carrying big sides of beef in the slaughterhouse must have made his arms really powerful.

In his younger days, Father was a bit of a Jack the Lad about town. Back in the twenties, when cars were a real novelty, he was one of the first young men in Hyde to have a car. It was a little white Austin Swallow sports car which he taught my mother to drive when she was only sixteen. It probably helped her decide that he was the man for her.

My mother was born Esther Shaw in 1910. Her father John came from quite a well to do family. I think the Shaws may have made their money in the cotton industry which was booming in Manchester in the 19th century. The Shaw family lived on a big estate called Denton Hall Farms. John's father, my great grandfather, owned a lot of properties around Manchester, and he used to go around collecting rents from them in his pony and trap. There was a family story that one day, as great grandfather was coming back with the rents, a man had jumped up on the trap and attacked him with a knife, trying to get the money. Great-grandfather had grabbed the robber's knife and slashed his hand, cutting off several fingers.

As a hobby he bred trotting ponies and would drive them in races himself. There was a trotting stadium at Droylesden, near Manchester, where he competed regularly, but he also used to take his ponies to race in France. So the family certainly wasn't short of a bob or two. But then almost overnight, the Shaws hit hard times.

Great grandfather was competing in a harness race somewhere one day when he fell off one of the little sulkies. The spectators thought he'd lost his balance and fallen, but when they went to help him, they discovered he'd had a heart attack and died. He was only in his early forties. Apparently his wife, my great grandmother, was an alcoholic, and after her husband died, some solicitors got hold of her in a drunken stupor and she signed away all the properties so my grandfather lost his inheritance.

As a result my grandfather never raced ponies himself, but as a boy he had watched his father compete. I remember a picture of his best pony Lilas, the one who raced in France, always hung in pride of place in my grandparents' front room. Grandfather used to work at the Droylesden harness track on race days, but it was nearly his undoing. One day he was manning the turnstile during a meeting when it was gate-crashed by some yobbos who tried to get in without paying. He went down under the heavy gate and his leg was broken very badly. In those days they used to set a leg straight rather than flexed, so when I was growing up I always remember him walking with a stiff leg and a limp.

My grandmother (my mother's mother) was born Mary Teresa Ashley. Her background was always a bit of a mystery. She came from Walsall, but would never tell anyone about her family. All we knew was that she was pregnant and left home. Whether she was kicked out in disgrace or ran away, I don't know to this day. The one thing she did tell me once was that she was a cousin to an opera singer called Sims Reeves. She had quite a nice voice herself and she used to sing a song called Bonny Jean which she said was one her cousin had made famous. I wasn't impressed. I'd never heard of Sims Reeves. I thought she was making him up. It was years later that I discovered Sims Reeves was not just an opera singer but the most famous British opera singer of the 19th century. So who knows? Maybe, through grandma, a few of the Sims Reeves genes made their way down to me and influenced the path my life took.

After leaving home Grandma had gone to work as a chambermaid in hotels, which is where she met my grandfather, and although he knew she was pregnant, he married her before the baby was born. Because of his lameness, grandfather was struggling to find work and as a way of earning a living, they took a pub in Flixton, which was little more than a village then, but which is now a very busy town on the outskirts of Manchester. It was called the Railway Inn Tavern, which I believe is still a pub today. After that first baby May, more and more children arrived, and many were given biblical names. My mother, Esther, was the fifth and after her there was one more, Abraham, always known as Abe. My mother had an elder brother called Harry. Harry had rather a tragic story. He caught pneumonia as a little boy and an elderly aunt used to come in and sit with him through the night so my grandmother could get a bit of rest. Next to the bed there was a bottle of medicine and a bottle of liniment to rub to Harry's chest, but one night the aunt was sleepy and mixed up the two bottles. Poor Harry swallowed a couple of tablespoons of liniment instead of medicine and as a result ended up brain-damaged. Even so, he grew up to be a talented artist, although he died quite young.

While mother was small, the family moved from Flixton to Mellor, at the edge of the Peak district where they ran a lovely old country pub called the Oddfellows Arms. It was quite remote and it was a very hard life. Grandma used to have to bring water up from the well and cook for all that big family on an open fire. She told me that she even used to feed the postman his breakfast early in the morning.

In those days, if people were ill. the local doctor would come up to the village on horseback. In winter however, being quite high up, the road to Mellor often used to be blocked with snow, so when people's babies were due in the village the doctor would tell them 'If I can't get to you, go and see Mrs Shaw, She's had six babies of her own. She'll deliver them'. She never actually trained as a nurse, but that was how grandmother came to act as the local midwife.

There was a well-known beauty spot near the Oddfellows Arms called Marple Lakes which had a big aqueduct close to it, carrying the Peak Forest canal across the river. It was a lovely area, where you could hire rowing boats on the lake. As a young girl, mother used to go down and hire a boat at weekends and one day she was rowing on the lake when some young men came crashing by in a rowing boat, larking about. One of them was my father, who was tipped into the lake and mother fished him out. And that was the start of it. He was ten years older than my mother and quite a dashing young man about town. Three years later, in December 1929, when mother was just nineteen, they were married.

Father and Mother moved around quite a bit when I was young. After my sister Patricia was born, two and a half years after me, Father bought different butcher's shops all around Manchester. But then, when I was about eight years of age, he suddenly decided he'd had enough of butchering and took a lovely big old pub called the Navigation Inn at Woodley where we all went to live. It was only about six miles from where my grandparent's had run their pub in Mellor (though by now they had retired) and after living until then in the heart of towns it seemed like heaven to Pat and me. The Navigation had a large garage attached to the car park. There were stables at the back, a stable yard and a big garden with a crown bowling green in it, where the locals used to play every week.

We had a very happy childhood in Woodley. Up till then we had never had pets, but after we moved to the Navigation we had dogs, cats, ponies, you name it. It was the beginning of my lifelong love of animals.

Our first pet was a lovely little dog called Snoopy. He was a mongrel and very friendly. Unfortunately, we didn't have him long before he came to a sad end. We had a big clubroom upstairs where my parents began hosting wedding receptions. They would book outside caterers to come in for the day to prepare the wedding breakfast. One day these caterers left a bucket of chicken bones by the back door. That night, poor little Snoopy got into the chicken bones and they pierced his intestines so he had to be put down. I was heartbroken. But it wasn't long before I said "Oh Dad Can we have another dog?"

Father didn't say yes, but he didn't say no either, so I started looking in the paper and one day I saw an advert for a puppy for sale somewhere in Manchester. When I told him about it, Dad said 'Oh well, all right. Get Tommy to take you and you can go and get it' (Tommy had a taxi business attached to the garage next door). Father gave me some cash and Tommy and I went off to Manchester and found the address, which was in a little back street.

I hadn't told dad what the pup was. It was a Great Dane! She was absolutely enormous. She was only about six months old but she was as big as a donkey. A half-starved donkey though. It was obvious the people who'd bought her couldn't afford to feed her properly. I fell in love immediately and handed over £26 in cash. In those days it was a lot of money, but the lady told me she was a pedigree and gave me her papers to prove it. She was called Slow Chloe of Gravel. So home I came in the taxi with Chloe, opened the door and found the family all sitting round the gate-leg table having tea. Chloe pushed past me, nearly knocking me over and ran straight under the table. The table went wallop and plates and knives went crashing everywhere. Everyone stood up in a panic and Father exclaimed 'My God, what's that you've got?'

'It's the puppy Dad' I said. For a terrible moment I thought he was going to make me take her back but in the end he weakened and soon Chloe became a much-loved member of our family. She was very funny. A year or two later, when I was practising singing, and doing my scales, she would howl the place down. You could hear her all through the village hollering. It was bedlam.

Soon after we moved into the Navigation Inn, my father bought my sister and me a little pony called Polly, with a governess cart thrown into the deal. Polly was a Russian pony and every winter she used to grow the most enormous thick coat so that she looked like a teddy bear. Pat and I both learned to ride and drive Polly, though she wasn't the most co-operative pony and could be feisty. Sometimes, when I was taking her out to the fields for a ride she would suddenly drop down and roll on me. It was horrible. I would be so winded I couldn't get my breath and thought I was dying. But it didn't put me off riding her. I always came back for more. Polly was involved in the biggest trouble I ever got into with my father.

The one thing I didn't like about living at the Navigation was the bowling green. As I got older, I had to mow the green and help my father worm it, by putting a special sand on the surface and watering it, which brought the worms to the surface. I also had to roll it regularly to keep the surface nice and smooth. There was a small roller and a big roller and the big one took quite a bit of pushing.

I got fed up with all this rollering and one day I had a bright idea. I fetched the harness from the governess cart, harnessed Polly to the big roller and drove her backwards and forwards over the green. Well, you can imagine. Polly was shod, so her hooves played absolute havoc with the beautiful crown green where they used to have competition matches. My father went mad. I was in his black books for quite a while.

Then one day I went to have a gallop through a nearby field which had a cinder track going through the middle of it. All at once, without any warning, Polly started bucking and I fell off while she was galloping and scraped my face badly in the cinders - it was a real gravel rash. The doctor came and plastered me in some sort of mustard poultice which set in a big scab. Days later, when it peeled off all the gravel came with it except for one little bit, which left a scar near my eye that I have to this day. After the doctor left, my father took one look at my face covered in poultice and said 'Right, that's it! That pony's got to go'.

So poor Polly was sold in disgrace. She went to a man Dad knew in the catering business called Fred Ibbotson. Fred had a bit of a drink problem and he had the bright idea of buying a pony and trap to take him to the pub so he wouldn't have to drive the car! I think Polly was quite happy in her new role. She obviously preferred being driven to being ridden!

By now both Pat and I were horse mad, and we kept on at Father to buy us another one. Eventually. one of my father's wheeler-dealer friends found an Irish horse that had just come off the boat. He was called Tommy. I think he had a bit of Shire in him because he was a great big heavy horse, but he was a gentle giant. I loved riding him, though I must have looked like a pimple on his back. I used to take him up to where they had levelled out a long strip of land ready to build a new road and gallop him across the soft ground. It made me feel like a knight on a charger. Tommy really could move. But he'd come from Ireland where he wasn't very used to traffic and that was the cause of another incident, which could have ended up even worse than my fall off Polly.

The main road in front of our pub was made of sets, which are flat cobbles, and they were criss-crossed with tramlines, because trams passed the front door as well, so traffic used to make quite a noise clattering over this road. By this time, it was the early forties and the war had started. There was some sort of army training camp near us, which had a lot of tanks and one day as I was taking Tommy for a ride, I saw one of these tank coming down the road towards us. If you can imagine the noise a tank made going over these sets, well it frightened me, never mind the horse!

Poor old Tommy was a gentle soul but he had never seen or heard anything like it. He started to shiver and shake, and then, utterly spooked, he bolted. Straight down the main road, straight through the traffic, hell for leather. It was terrifying. I just couldn't stop him. Fortunately, I managed to hang on like a limpet until eventually he ran out of puff and calmed down. Neither of us was any the worse for the ordeal, but after that I kept my ears open and if I ever heard the noise of tanks when I was out for a ride, I'd turn tail and get off the road as quickly as I could.

Seeing how keen Pat and I were, Father sent us to have some lessons at a nearby riding school. They had a very beautiful pony there that everyone wanted to ride but they would only let the more experienced riders get on him because he was a bit too lively for beginners. Because of our experience with Polly and Tommy, both Pat and I were considered good enough to ride Tinker and we took a shine to him. Realising that, Father did a deal with the riding school owner, who took Tommy who was so quiet and gentle, although he was so big, and in exchange he gave us Tinker.

Tinker proved to be a much more suitable mount than Tommy for small girls and I used to ride him every spare moment I had until I left school. Later, when I left home, my sister Pat took over and rode him very successfully in show competitions. She even rode him in a pageant once, riding side-saddle. He was a wonderful pony. Sadly, a few years later when my parents left the pub, they had nowhere to keep him, so he had to be sold.

The tanks that frightened Tommy weren't the only thing that reminded us there was a war on. At the end of 1940 there were a lot of air raids over Manchester. They called it the Christmas Blitz. We had a big cellar in the pub with electric lights and a big boiler and Father put a bed and chairs in the cellar so that when the sirens went we could all go down.

Pat and I used to sleep in a big double bed together upstairs and we would lie awake at night waiting for the sirens to go. We thought it was great fun and I used to say 'Oh listen to the aeroplanes Pat'. We got to know that the sound of the engines of English planes was different from the sound of the German planes. 'Pat! It's a Gerry, come on!' I'd say. And we'd jump out of bed, put on our dressing gowns and slippers and fly downstairs to the cellar. By this time Mother was very pregnant with Ann our little sister and she used to make us cocoa to take down into the cellar with us.

One night, just before Christmas when I was ten and Pat was six, the sirens went. We came downstairs and were sitting in a big armchair together waiting for our cocoa and watching the old men in the bar playing dominoes. Mother had just us made us a drink of cocoa and was carrying it towards us when Woof! a bomb fell, somewhere very close to the pub. All the heavy Britannia tables, with their iron bases and big wooden tops, bounced up in the air and dominoes flew everywhere. All the lights went out, and the doors either flew open or slammed shut. All the windows broke, there was glass all over the place. Mother threw herself on top of us, with the big coat she was wearing spread wide to cover us and shield us from the glass.

In a panic, we all rushed blindly down to the cellar. All the poor old men who'd been playing dominoes followed. It was pitch dark downstairs but Dad kept a supply of candles in the cellar for emergencies and managed to find them and light them. As the candlelight light flickered, Pat and I looked across at mother and saw that she was covered in cocoa. We started giggling our heads off. We thought it was hilarious, but, we were the only ones who did. The old men were crying, thinking their houses had gone up in smoke and Mother and Father looked very shocked. But we didn't register that. We just couldn't stop laughing. And what happened next nearly sent us into hysterics.

It was very nearly Christmas time and we had ordered a turkey from some butchers. Minutes after the bomb fell, the delivery man arrived at the pub with the turkey to find the place all in darkness, with smoke everywhere, and all the windows were blown in. He stuck his head through a broken window in the lounge and shouted down to us 'Is there anybody there?' which sent Pat and me into more fits of giggles. We had no idea that we might have all been killed. Anyway, the man delivered the turkey and despite the broken windows we were all able to celebrate Christmas.

Father wasn't called up to fight in the war-partly because at 39, he was a bit too old, but also because he was a master butcher, which was a reserved occupation. It meant he had to go back to butchering for the local Co-op while my mother ran the pub. The income from butchering was very welcome because like other businesses in the war years, the pub was badly hit by rationing. Some days we weren't even able to open the pub because there was no beer- a month's ration of beer used to be delivered in one go and when it was gone, it was gone.

Because of rationing there was quite a thriving black market and people would barter goods like backyard eggs and home grown vegetables for coupons. I suspect Dad was able to exchange a bit of meat from his butchering for extras and treats for mother and Pat and me.

Extras were especially welcome in the early years of the war as our family had grown again. In 1941, a month or so after the air raid near-miss, my youngest sister Anne arrived. Just before she was born, Mother got a bladder infection and had to go into hospital. She told us that while she was there the nurses made her drink eight pints of barley water every day and forever afterwards she used to feel sick at the sight of the barley water.

When Anne eventually arrived and Pat and I were taken to see our new sister in hospital, we weren't at all impressed. Poor Anne was so wrinkled and shrivelled up we thought she looked just like a prune. Mother was forced to agree, but blamed it on the barley water!

CHAPTER 2

Although the war years were hard, Dad had done very well in the pub in the time leading up to the war and had put money aside for our education.

Soon after Anne was born, I was sent as a day pupil to the Convent of the Nativity at Romiley, near Stockport, which was a boarding school run by nuns. Two years later Pat followed me there. The convent gave us a good education, but the nuns were very strict and as I was a bit of a rebel, I didn't go down too well with them. I always seemed to be in trouble for one thing or another, usually without intending to do anything wrong.

The worst incident I remember happened the first Christmas soon after I started there. I learned that it was a tradition for the girls to club together to give a Christmas present to their form teacher. Our form teacher was called Miss Tricket and nobody seemed to have any idea what to give her until I came up with a bright idea. During the war, you couldn't get a bottle of whisky for love or money but I knew that father had a secret supply for friends so I said 'I know. I'll pay dad and we'll give Miss Tricket a bottle of whisky'. So that's what we did.

When Sister Hilda, the head teacher, found out, all hell broke loose. The whisky was returned to my father, I was threatened with expulsion and I was called before Sister Hilda to explain myself.

She glared at me "What were you thinking of child, giving a teacher whisky?"

'I thought she'd be jolly glad of it' I said. I genuinely couldn't understand what the fuss was about.

And yet they had the nerve a year or two later when Sister Superior was on her deathbed to call me in and say 'Could you possibly get us a little brandy for her?' Honestly! So that rather put me against the Catholic religion and nuns for life.

From very early on I was a natural show-off and had always loved performing in front of people. Even when I was quite small, I would burst into song at the drop of a hat and was always happy to perform party pieces at Christmas. At my new school I started taking piano lessons which gave me even more opportunities to perform.

In my early teens father came across some ladies who ran a dance academy in Hyde and decided to enrol Pat and me for dancing lessons as well. The academy used to do a concert at the end of every term and when they found I could sing as well as dance, I was always the leading light up in front of the other dancers on stage, singing and strutting my stuff. They used to make us costumes out of blackout cloth and yellow dusters. It was great fun. But that's all. I don't think it ever crossed my mind at this stage that I might make a career out of performing.

It was my grandmother who was responsible for encouraging me in that direction, though she didn't realise it at the time. My grandparents retired and gave up the Oddfellows Arms when I was quite young and had moved to a 3 storey weaver's cottage in Mellor. When grandfather died a couple of years later my grandmother didn't like living on her own and because she missed the pub life, she used to come and stay with us during the week to help out. She was a very good cook, and as well as putting dinner on the table for the whole family most days, she would make us girls lovely home—made toffee. Then at weekends she would go back to her cottage and she and her friend Mrs Duckworth, used to go to the local pub, The Royal Oak. Grandma was very fond of me, the eldest one and used to take me back with her to Mellor at weekends which meant I was allowed to accompany them to the pub. This was a big occasion and we would all smarten ourselves up for it. I can see her now; Grandmother used to have curling tongs which she warmed up in the oven. In those day I had long blonde hair, which she would put in curls and ringlets. Then she would start on her own hair, but often she'd be so busy talking to me that she'd forget to take the tongs out and I'd have to shout 'Grandma, your hair's singeing!' There were nearly always brown steaks in her grey hair where she'd left the tongs in too long.

We used to sit in the back roof the pub, which was called the parlour, where I would be given grapefruit juice and crisps while Grandma and her friend had a Guinness before going onto the whiskies. When Pat got a bit older she used to come with us and we'd both spend our weekends in Mellor, which must have given my parents more time when the Navigation was at its busiest.

My grandmother's next door neighbour in Mellor took in lodgers and her first guests were two middle-aged sisters whose surname was Wood. They were both spinsters, like a lot of women of that generation, because so many young men had been killed in the first world war. One of these ladies was called Winifred. She was an artist and had a little studio in the orchard across the road where she used to give painting lessons. The other sister had been a missionary out in

China—I never learned her real name and I used to call her Miss China Wood. She'd toured China with a donkey and a young boy. She fascinated me because, even though she looked like quite an old lady, she was still able to sit cross-legged on the floor. She could also paint Chinese letters, and she had really beautiful silk kimonos.

Every Saturday morning Pat and I used to go to the children's cinema show in Marple. Afterwards, I would come back to Mellor and tell the Wood sisters stories from the films and sing all the songs from the musicals to amuse them. They were a very appreciative audience, and our weekend concerts became a regular thing. I used to make Pat join in, though she wasn't nearly as keen as me on performing, but I was the typical older sister and a bit bossy, so she didn't have much choice.

One day, soon after I started at the convent school, and unknown to me, Winifred went to see my parents. 'You know you really ought to have Joan's voice trained' she told them. 'She has a very good singing voice'.

If she'd left it at that, they might have thought she was just being polite and wouldn't have done anything about it. But then she added 'I know a bit about music, because I'm the cousin of Sir Henry Wood'.

That did it! Henry Wood had started The Proms, as the London promenade concerts were known, back in 1895 and was still conducting them during the second world war when he was well into his seventies. The Proms had been in the news recently because in 1941 the Queen's Hall in London, where they were held, had been bombed, but Sir Henry Wood had announced that rather than letting the Germans stop them, the concerts would move to the Royal Albert Hall. Every year, as long as I could remember, both my parents had listened to the Promenade concerts on the radio. So Sir

Henry was looked on as a bit of a hero in our house and Father decided to take notice of Miss Wood's advice. There and then, it was decided that as well as piano lessons, I should start having private singing lessons at the convent school.

My first singing teacher was a lovely Irish lady called Oona Slevin. She had been a professional singer and violinist, but had suffered some sort of a breakdown so had come to the school to teach. We got on like a house on fire. I worshipped her. She had a lovely voice and would often demonstrate how to sing a new song herself instead of just telling me what to do. I would imitate her slavishly, which sometimes had unintended consequences.

One day, one of my aunts took me to sing for somebody that she knew and he asked me to sing a song that I absolutely detested. It was called 'A brown bird singing' and it was frightfully English. I sang it, but moaned about it and told the man I didn't like it. 'But you sang it beautifully dear'. he said. 'The only thing is you sang it with an Irish accent!'

At that time, we used to have some very handsome Irish doctors who met at the pub every Friday night. One was a resident surgeon at Stockport infirmary; another was at Manchester Royal and they used to have a little drinking session and stay on quite late. I was madly in love with one of them, Paddy Delaney, a big strapping fellow with freckles and fair hair. I think it was the start of my lifelong weakness for Irishmen!

I mentioned to Miss Slevin that we had some Irish doctors coming into the pub and she and another Irish teacher were all agog to meet these young men, though they were a bit nervous about coming into the pub on their own. I said 'Oh you ought to come. It's all right. I'll be there too (on a Friday night I was allowed to stay up till quite late). So they came into the pub the following Friday and were soon having a great time with the doctors.

Unfortunately, the word got out at school and the nuns hauled both the teachers in on Monday and gave them a real dressing down 'Don't you go to the pub. It's not the thing to do' and so on. So I was in disgrace over that too.

Soon after that, not surprisingly, poor Miss Slevin decided she'd had enough of the nuns and left the school, and another music teacher came along, a Miss Caroll. She was also Irish, but unlike Miss Slevin she was a nasty piece of work, with a real Irish paddy on her. Even worse, she couldn't sing for toffee! After just a few lessons I went home and told my parents 'I can't work with her. I can't carry on with this Miss Caroll. I'm just not learning anything from her.' We were having piano lessons from her as well, so both my piano lessons and singing lessons came to an abrupt halt.

Poor Pat always blamed me for the end of her own musical education. She said 'I was doing very well you know with my piano lessons with Miss Caroll but she was so annoyed when you packed in that she took it out on me'. Pat used to learn her pieces off by heart and one day she had turned over two pages but carried on playing because she knew what came next. Miss Caroll picked up a ruler and rapped poor Pat's knuckles and told her off because she said she should be reading the music. Pat came home crying that day and that was the end of her lessons too!

Then mother said 'Well we'll have to sort out some more singing lessons for Joan' because I was doing quite well with it. As a result of Miss Slevin's teaching I sang all the leads at the school plays and at the school Christmas concert, I used always to be the soloist for the carols.

It was an unlikely chain of events which led to my next teacher. Before she met my father, my mother had a boyfriend known as Ginger Pashley. He'd been a dirt track rider at Belleview, which was a big pleasure park like Blackpool. Belleview had a funfair with a big dipper, a large concert hall, where they had classical concerts and boxing matches, and a zoo and gardens — it was quite a place. And of course they also had this famous dirt track where they used to hold the racing. In her teens, mother would go around riding pillion on Ginger's motorbike and he had taken her on the back of his bike to meet his family in Manchester. To her surprise, it turned out that Ginger was the black sheep of the family. The rest of them were musicians and singers. Mother said that when she first went through the door into his house, someone was playing the violin, someone was having singing lessons and someone else was on the piano. It was a real musical set-up.

Mother got to know all the family and stayed in touch with them even after she broke off with Ginger and married Dad. Ginger's sister Anita Pashley married the leader of the Halle orchestra, Stuart Knusson. She and Stuart had two boys, who both grew up to be musicians when they came out of the army. One of those boys, Stuart Junior, later had a son, Oliver Knusson, who was a child prodigy. He wrote an opera when he was 12 and became a famous composer.

While her sons were still quite young, Anita split up from Stuart and came back to Mellor (the family must have had roots in Mellor). She opened some little tea-rooms at the top of the village up on the hillside behind Mellor Church and mother used to go and visit her there. One day when mother was at the tearooms she mentioned to Anita about me and my problems with Miss Caroll and Anita said 'Oh bring her to me. I'll give her singing lessons.' So that was that. I went to

Anita for lessons for the next couple of years until I started my final year at school.

During that time, I started to perform quite a lot in public locally. This also had something to do with the Irish doctors! One day a lady knocked on the pub door and asked in a strong Welsh accent to speak to Miss Booth. Out I came in my gymslip and she said 'Have you finished with your library book dear, because if you have, I want to read it' I went a bit red. I was a member of the local library and I used to take out books of plays to act out in the barn at home. I often used to hang on to them for far too long. While I went to fetch the book, my father started talking to the lady and learned that her name was Kay Browning. She was a teacher and her husband was away fighting in the war. He was one of the Desert Rats, serving in North Africa and poor Mrs Browning had no idea when she would see him next. Realising that she was a bit lonely, my father said 'Why don't you come up and have a drink in the pub one evening?'. She told him she'd like to very much, but like Miss Slevin she was nervous about coming into the pub on her own. So Dad said 'Oh you should come up on Friday evenings. we have some very nice doctors who come here'.

Kate Browning started to come to these Friday evening sessions with her cousin and as luck would have it, she turned out to be a very good pianist. She would sit down at the bar's old upright piano and we would have great sing-songs with me leading the singing and the doctors and father joining in.

Kay was a teacher at Leigh Street School in Hyde and she invited me to sing at her school concert, where she played the piano to accompany me. I sang One Fine Day from Madame Butterfly on that first occasion. It went down well and it wasn't long before the two of us were being asked to perform at other concerts. One day Kay persuaded me to enter the

Carol Leavis radio talent show, The Discovery Show. We went to a big cinema near Stockport and I sang my party piece for him, Il Bacio, a difficult colorata number. I followed it up with Sitting in the Noonday Sun, a negro spiritual, of all things. I had so much confidence as a child! would get up anywhere and sing anything! Carol Leavis liked me and I was selected to appear in The Discovery Show at the cinema that night.

After the war finished, Kay's husband Bob, returned and started coming to the pub too. He and Kay later became great friends of my parents.

In 1946 I sat my school certificate, (now called GCSE's). I did well and the nuns wanted me to stay on at school and go to University. I agreed to take my Higher School Certificate but as for university, I wasn't having any of it. 'I don't want to go to University' I said. 'I want to sing. I want to go on the stage.'

The nuns were horrified, but my parents were much more understanding. They knew how important singing had become to me and I think they had always suspected the way I was heading! They asked Anita for advice over what to do next.

'To be honest I feel I've gone as far as I can with Joan', she told Father. 'She needs somebody now with more professional experience'.

Anita recommended two teachers in Manchester who she thought might be suitable. One was Lilian Stiles-Allen, an operatic soprano (who later taught Julie Andrews) who she said was very good technically, but her preference was for Frank Mullings, who had been the lead tenor at the Royal Opera house when Sir Thomas Beecham ran Covent Garden.

Anita said he was noted for his acting ability, specialising in all the dramatic Wagnerian stuff.

So when I was about seventeen, I started having private lessons with Frank Mullings. It was a totally new experience and I loved it. Frank Mullings was a very big man, with an even bigger voice and a very strong personality. He had a thick mane of hair and walked with a bit of a stagger, because once, when he'd been appearing in an opera, he had put his foot in a hole on the stage and damaged his Achilles tendon.

The famous Manchester Guardian music critic Neville Cardus, raved about Frank Mullings, He wrote 'You had to see Mullings perform. There was some criticism of aspects of his voice, but he was such a strong actor that you could always believe what he was singing'.

It was this acting ability that made a great impression on me from the word go. His diction was perfect. If he sang a little English song it was absolutely beautiful — it sounded as if he was reading poetry.

Frank Mullings taught me new techniques, and from him I learned operatic arias and much more serious and difficult stuff than I had ever sung before. Apart from giving private lessons, Mr Mullings taught both at the Royal College in Manchester and the Birmingham School of Music. Soon after I took my Higher School Certificate, knowing that I was going to leave school soon, he said 'Joan, there's a scholarship for a singer at the Manchester College coming up. I think you should apply for it'.

I had dreamed of going to the Royal College for a long time. I knew that my parents couldn't afford to send me there as the fees were quite high, and by now, because of rationing, the catering side of the business had dried up and the supply of beer was still limited, so the pub had gone downhill. In

1948 father was still having to do private butchering to make ends meet. The chance of a scholarship was like an answer to my prayers.

A few weeks later I went to the audition at the Royal College. I had to sing three pieces. The first was an English ballad. Next, I sang in French (thanks to the nuns I had a good French accent). It was a very tricky little song by Debussy, which I had mastered quite well. Finally, I sang an operatic aria. My performance was very well received and Frank Mullings was delighted with me. 'You'll walk this' he said. 'You're far in advance of anyone else who has applied'. I thought I was home and dry.

But I wasn't. The scholarship was given to a boy. Mr Mullings was convinced it was because the head of the college was his uncle. 'It's quite ridiculous' he fumed when he told me.

He was so disgusted and furious at the outcome that he resigned from the college, and from then on just taught privately. I carried on as a private pupil of his for a few more months with little idea of what I would do next. My Higher School Certificate results came out and I learned that I had done very well. Once again the nuns tried to persuade me to go to University, but I refused. Instead, I decided to audition for local amateur musicals while I waited for another professional opportunity to turn up.

My first amateur stage part was in a musical comedy called Mr Cinders with the Hyde Amateur Light Opera Company, when I played a character called Phyllis. Frank Mullings came to see the first night. My mother also came to witness my debut and after the show, brought Frank Mullings back to the pub where my grandmother was waiting to collar him.

'Oh, you're from Walsall' she said. 'I'm from Walsall too'. They started chatting together and putting on silly Birmingham accents.

Suddenly I heard her say to Frank Mullings 'Well you know, Mr Mullings I'm related to the great Sims Reeves'. I tried desperately to get her to shut up! 'Mr Mullings won't have heard of him Grandma' I said.

Frank Mullings frowned at me. 'Never heard of him Joan? Of course I've heard of the great Sims Reeves'. He turned back to Grandma 'Madame it's an honour to meet you 'he said, bowing theatrically. Grandma, of course, was delighted.

The next day, when I went for my singing lesson Frank Mullings pointed up at his bookshelf. 'Get down that Encyclopaedia of British Music Joan' he instructed 'And read about your illustrious ancestor!'

I obeyed and was suitably astonished. Apparently, Sims Reeves had written many books on the Bel Canto method of singing. He was also a leading tenor at La Scala, Milan in the 19th century. He was a real celebrity of the day, who travelled with his own doctor and chef and goodness knows what, and when he came back to England there was always a hero's welcome. Frank Mullings said he could remember as a boy seeing big posters saying 'Welcome home Sims Reeves'. 'And you, he said to me are related to him. Not many people can say that. If ever you find yourself nervous in an audition, just remember your family connections!

For the next few months I carried on appearing in local amateur shows while I thought about what to do next. For a short while It looked as though I would get a second chance at a professional career when the Carl Rose Opera company came to Manchester. The company was run by an elderly lady called Mrs Phillips. Frank Mullings knew her well and he arranged for me to go and meet and sing for her. When Mrs Phillips heard me, possibly because I was very slim when I was 18, and looked a bit boyish, she said instantly 'Oh yes, she'd make a beautiful Cherubino in the Marriage of Figaro' (Cherubino is supposed to be a young boy but is always played by a girl).

'She must learn the part of Cherubino. She will be perfect.' Mrs Phillips said.

I was so thrilled; I was going to start my singing career with an opera company! But damn me didn't Mrs Phillips die soon afterwards and the whole Carl Rosa opera company went into liquidation and was no more. Maybe, I thought, I just wasn't meant to go in opera.

Finally, fate decided to be kind to me. In the summer of 1949 a show called Lilac Time came to the Palace Theatre in Manchester. Lilac Time was an operetta rather than a musical. It was based on the life of Schubert and consisted of Schubert's music with lyrics set to it. It toured for many years in the late forties and fifties and was a great success.

One of the artists in the show was an ex pupil of Frank Mullings and while the company was in Manchester he came along for some lessons, bringing with him an Irish singer called Joe Seely. I was waiting for my own lesson there one day and overheard Joe Seely singing in the next room. I remember thinking that he had the most beautiful bass voice I'd ever heard.

After they left and I went in for my lesson Frank Mullings said 'Joan, I think it's time you had some professional experience'. He told me that he'd arranged for me to go to the Palace Theatre to do an audition.

After my recent disappointments I didn't allow myself to get my hopes up, but I went along obediently, and to my surprise and delight, after they'd heard me sing, I was offered a job in the chorus in Emile Littler's forthcoming tour of Lilac Time.

My professional stage life was launched at last!

CHAPTER 3

I hadn't yet learned to drive, so early in 1949 my mother took me down on the train to London and we stayed at a small hotel for a week or so while I joined the rest of the cast for rehearsals in an old church hall in Holborn.

Lilac Time was the ideal show for me to start my stage career because everyone in it was a trained singer, so the standards were high. It was a really good musical and very popular in those days, though you never hear of it now. Like the Merry Widow and others of its kind it has disappeared almost without trace.

Most of the cast had appeared in Lilac Time in the previous season and knew the score back to front, so it only took ten days of rehearsal before we were ready to set off on tour. Our first opening was at the New Theatre in Hull.

I was very green and naïve and had never been away from home before, so to me, touring was a dream world, full of new, eye-opening experiences. I loved travelling in trains from town to town, staying in digs, and dressing in lovely costumes every night. Lilac Time was set in the early 19th century, so we had to have ringlets and bonnets and bustles and wear long frilly trousers under our skirts and carry parasols.

One of the many new skills I had to learn was putting on the heavy stage make-up and taking it off again after the show using the famous Crowes Cremine vanishing cream

(something I use to this day and which people tell me has kept my skin in very good condition for someone my age!)

For a young girl not long out of Convent school it was all very new and exciting. And not just the performing part. Offstage, I was pursued by Mr Joe Seely, the basso profundo. He made passes at me all the time. I had already fallen in love with his voice when I'd heard him having a music lesson in Manchester. It was really superb. The amazing thing about his talent was that it was completely natural: he wasn't conventionally musical in the sense that he didn't read music, and he was virtually self-taught. Those lessons he'd had with Frank Mullings had been quite a novelty for him.

On top of Joe's impressive singing ability, he was a very, very charming man, with that typical Irish twinkle in his eyes for which I'd always had a soft spot. So when he started pursuing me, it had to be only a matter of time before I succumbed. Just before the end of the tour, the inevitable happened. We were in digs together in Plymouth where Joe Seely had a room upstairs and I had a room downstairs. During the last week of the tour, he came down in the middle of the night and crept into bed with me. So I lost my virginity in Plymouth at the age of 19. (Sadly, I have to say it wasn't a particularly memorable occasion!)

My relationship with Joe Seely turned out to be short-lived. All the theatres used to do a pantomime at Christmas so we had to stop the tour for the whole of the pantomime season. During our final week in Plymouth the company went out to entertain the sailors on the USS Hamul, which was an American ship anchored in the harbour and we had a great time.

After we came ashore, because the cast was going to split up, Celia Lipton, who was a famous singer and film actress in the fifties and the star of the show, had arranged an end of season party for the cast at a restaurant in Plymouth. Everything, including the food and drink was laid on and we were all having a great time until, unfortunately, Joe Sealy got very drunk. It turned out he was one of these Irishmen that when they'd had a drink, wanted to fight. He was a big heavy man, six foot odd and well-built and he started a brawl in the middle of the restaurant and practically wrecked the place. Tables and chairs were smashed, glasses broken, the whole thing. Poor Celia Lipton had to go back the next day and pay for the damage and sort it all out.

We had never gone out drinking while we were on tour and performing every night, so I hadn't seen that side of Joe before and of course. it put me right off him. I felt shell-shocked. What a week it had been! So much had happened to me in seven short days. I couldn't wait to get home!

When I did get back to Woodley that November of 1949, I immediately started looking for more work to tide me through the winter season until Lilac Time opened again in the spring. Through Frank Mullings I heard that a repertory company in Manchester called Chorlton cum Hardy Rep was putting on a pantomime, Dick Whittington, in Manchester. Frank Mulling's son Peter, a young man who I had got to know while Frank was teaching me, was the stage manager for the show, while a Manchester composer of popular type music, called Alan Ferguson, had written all the songs. Apparently Jack Hylton, the impresario, had expressed an interest, so the company decided to put Dick Whittington on just for a short season, with a view to letting Jack Hylton hear Alan Ferguson's music and maybe picking the show up and taking the repertory company on to bigger things.

All the cast of the pantomime were regular actors and actresses who could sing a bit if required, but there was one particular song that Alan Ferguson had written called 'Sunrise', which needed a trained voice.

Apparently, without telling me, Peter had told them 'Oh Joan's coming back at Christmas. She can do it.' So without even giving me an audition, they put me into the pantomime and I was given just a couple of weeks to learn my part.

My big scene took place in the middle of the show where half the cast were shipwrecked. The scene opened on a tropical island with a lot of children dancing to a number called 'Somewhere in Hawaii' Quite how the writers made that tie in with the Dick Whittington story I can't remember. All the scenery was painted with luminous paint to suggest tropical light and I was dressed in a sarong and tied to a palm tree. From this rather uncomfortable position I had to sing 'Sunrise'. It was quite a good ballad, which afterwards Josef Locke, the Irish singer, took up and made very popular.

One of the members of Chorlton Rep at that time was Harry Corbett (later of Steptoe and Son fame). He was a virtual unknown then and hadn't yet added the 'H' in the middle of his name to distinguish him from the Harry Corbett who performed with Sooty the glove puppet. Harry was engaged to Avis Bunnage, the actress playing the principal girl. Later on, Avis became quite a well-known character actor, although she and Harry never did get married. Harry had quite a good voice and sang a song later on in the show called Sidney the Spiv, which he did in a cockney accent while dressed as a barrow boy.

In the shipwreck scene, Harry played a native—he used to paint potassium permanganate on his skin to make him look brown. He had to sit playing bongo drums at my feet while I was tied to the palm tree singing. Harry had a wicked sense of humour and he used to take it as a challenge to try and make me laugh during my song. Very often in rehearsals he succeeded. My sarong had fringes on which would suddenly start shaking uncontrollably and I would end up in fits of giggles hardly able to sing a word. The director would say 'For God's sake Harry, stop making her laugh. All the scenery's shaking'.

It turned out that Jack Hylton did like the show and I believe he helped Alan Ferguson get some of his music published.

After Dick Whittington came to the end of its run I re-joined the company of Lilac Time as it started another tour. Joe was still playing a principal role as one of the three jolly brothers, but our relationship had cooled off after his drunken antics at the end of the last tour. (Despite that experience however, I still hadn't been cured of my weakness for the Irish. I don't know why, but there you are.)

The second tour lasted for six months and afterwards, I went home again to Woodley.

Shortly afterwards, while I was browsing through the Stage magazine, which was where all forthcoming auditions were advertised, I spotted an ad for a job with the National Light Opera Company. They were about to set off on tour and were rotating three different operettas: Merrie England, Chu Chin Chow and Lilac Domino. The format was to do three days of one show then end the week with the second one and start the next week with the third, shuffling them all about. It needed a big cast and was quite a demanding schedule, so people often dropped out, which meant that from time to time they ran out of singers. I went along to the audition to try my luck and was offered a place in the chorus. Soon afterwards I joined the NLOC on their new tour.

My experience in the two productions of Lilac Time gave me an advantage and for the first time I got to understudy one of the main parts. On one memorable night, the star of Lilac Domino wasn't very well and I did actually get to sing the lead role of Georgine, the masked young girl who steals the heart of a count at a masquerade ball in Nice.

I toured with the National Light Opera Company for quite some time. The company was run and produced by Ralph Reader, the man who ran the famous 'Gang Shows' in London. Many of the principals and nearly all the chorus in Ralph Reader's shows were openly gay. I had never encountered gays before so it was quite an education for me.

I remember one funny old chap in the chorus who must have been about ninety. Everyone in the show used to call him 'the old queen'. There was also a long standing couple in the company. One of them, Billy, looked like a boxer—he was very thick-set—but the moment he opened his mouth he was really camp. He was very interested in women's clothes and would always compliment you on your outfits. His partner, who was tall, thin and dark had been the understudy in films for Humphrey Bogart and looked a bit like him. The two of them had an apartment in London which, I was told by people who'd seen it, was out of this world and beautifully furnished with lots of lovely antiques.

Billy used to sell high quality stage make up to the rest of the cast as a side-line. His dressing room was always packed full of jars and bottles. But it was also equipped with a stove and a little table covered with a cloth and laid out with a china tea service.' 'Would you like a cup of tea dear?' were always his first words to anyone like me who knocked on his door wanting to buy make-up.

In the years to come, I was to encounter many gay men in show business and always got on very well with them. The ones I met were usually artistic and loved the company of women. I found they were often much more complimentary than straight men about your hairstyle, clothes and general appearance!

I had my 21st birthday party during the English Light Opera company tour. I was performing in Plymouth in Choo Chin Chow that weekend and my parents came down for two days, bringing a load of food from the pub with them. We took a room in the pub next door to the theatre. I was a bit worried because the long bar there was a famous place for rough and tumble but they let us have a room upstairs. The conductor of the orchestra came and played the piano for me and we all danced and had a bit of a sing-song. My parents gave me a watch. It was a lovely evening. Between one thing and another I have a few lasting memories of Plymouth!

By now I had another romance in my life. One week during the tour's early weeks we had found ourselves in digs in Northampton. There was a young doctor staying in the same digs and he invited one of the girls from the show out with him and asked if I'd make up a foursome with a friend of his. Of course I said yes. The friend turned out to be a rather charming Irish doctor, very tall, good-looking and funny, called John Laing. He was from Limerick and was working as a locum in Northampton. We became good friends during the week I was in Northampton and after the tour moved on we used to write to each other and speak on the telephone a couple of times a week. Because he was a locum, John moved about the country a lot but we used to meet up occasionally when I had a day off.

One day he rang to tell me he had taken a locum position in Birmingham near the Aston Villa football ground. When I said that I was on my way to auditions in London the next week he invited me to call in at Birmingham on my way and stay with him. I did, and that's when we became an 'item' as we used to say in those days. I really liked him. He was witty and he played the guitar and he was good fun. But of course he was all over the place because he was doing locum jobs and I was all over the country performing in different theatres with the national Light Opera Company so it was never going to work in the long run.

Later that year John decided he wanted to go back to Ireland to take another degree and try to become a consultant. We used to phone each other often while he was in Ireland. But it didn't work out for him there for some reason and he came back to London after a couple of months.

His mother had gone to live in America and she owned a great big house in Ealing, but when she left the country she had divided it up and let it out. All the ground floor was let off as a big apartment while John and his brother shared the first floor apartment. When our tour reached the South of England I used to go and stay with John in London quite a lot.

It was a magnificent house. The ground floor was very elegant with a grand staircase. The upstairs, with two young men living there wasn't quite so impressive. The kitchen was always a bit of a mess!

When our affair came to an end, I'm afraid it was thanks to my old mate Joe Sealy. He was a regular in the cast of the Exeter Christmas pantomime and one day towards the end of that NLOC tour, he phoned me up and said 'Are you interested in playing Dandini in Cinderella at Exeter this year because they're looking for somebody?'

Of course I said yes. Work was work! Unfortunately, that didn't go down too well with John Laing. When I told him that I was going to Exeter and that Joe was in the cast he said 'Oh that Joe Sealy again!' I'd told him about our earlier relationship and he thought I was still interested in him. I wasn't, but it looked a bit that way I suppose, because our paths kept crossing. Soon after that, John found a more permanent job somewhere further away and we just lost touch with each other.

That Christmas, after the tour closed, I followed up on Joe Sealy's suggestion and took up the panto job as Dandini at Exeter. I was beginning to get a taste for pantomime, although I missed having Christmas at home with my family. It paid reasonably well and the costumes and choreography were fun. I made the most of it. After all, if Covent Garden wanted me to sing opera, it was unlikely I'd be doing panto ever again!

The following year, 1952, I toured again with the English Light Opera company, singing in three new shows. But they weren't quite as successful. One of the shows was 'Waltzes from Vienna' which was all Strauss's music. The other one was called 'The Lisbon Story'. The theme tune for which, 'Pedro the Fisherman', became very famous. The action took place in Lisbon when it was occupied by Germany, and the leading lady was a spy working against the Nazis. There was a scene where somebody was shot and I was in the crowd looking on. One thing I had always been terrified was loud bangs. I couldn't stand fireworks. Every night I used to be wound up like a coiled spring until the gun had gone off. It used to put me through hell.

CHAPTER 4

Just before the second National Light Opera Tour finished. I auditioned for a job in an Anthony Goodson review called 'A Christmas Carnival'. The production advertised itself as 'a cross between pantomime and circus' which sounded exciting, but definitely wasn't! It turned out to be a really tatty review with several matinee performances and a small cast spread very thinly which meant I was on stage a lot. We toured out of season holiday resorts ending up on the pier in Scarborough. The audiences were sparse and the reception was poor, which was depressing. For the first time ever I found myself wondering if I had made a mistake in choosing a stage career. When I found myself in cold and dingy digs in Scarborough on Christmas eve, I phoned home in tears. My parents were so worried about me that my father sent a friend with his car all the way to Scarborough to fetch me home so I could spend Christmas Day with my family.

To my relief the show petered out and its run ended prematurely. I returned home and was once more scrutinising The Stage for job opportunities when, out of the blue, Joe Sealy called me and told me that Leon Underwood was putting on a new production of Lilac Time and he could organise an audition for me.

The show had become an old friend by now. I loved the music and knew it backwards. My audition must have impressed Leon Underwood because for the first time I found myself promoted from the chorus and offered the part of Willi, one of the three sisters. I was also appointed understudy for the lead soprano role of Lili, the youngest sister, who played the love of Schubert's life. I was coming up in the world!

In this production Lilli and Schubert were being played by two Australian singers. Joe Sealy was also in the cast, singing his usual role of Schwind, one of the three jolly brothers who were friends of Schubert. One of the other brothers sang one of the show's big songs 'Hark, Hark, the lark' in harmony with him. Joe was still keen on me but I wouldn't have anything to do with him. We were friends, but that was it. Oh no. keep away from me Joe! Even so, I did try and help him with his career.

His agent had arranged an audition at Covent Garden. The Opera company were very much impressed with his voice and told him to learn the role of Sorastro from the Magic Flute. During our tour I started giving Joe lessons because he had this wonderful voice and I thought he could really go into serious opera if he had more musical knowledge. We hired a studio for an hour or two and I taught him to sing Sorastro's two arias. Sorastro was a real bass part which suited him perfectly, but after a while in my heart I realised that with his Irish accent and the fact that he couldn't read music and his drinking, he was unlikely to become a star. But the main reason was that he just wasn't committed enough. In the end he didn't even bother to return to Covent Garden when he was called and all my effort was wasted.

It was typical of Joe. That was what was so silly. He always got jobs when he auditioned. At one stage he had actually won an understudy part in the hit West End musical South Pacific. But he hadn't bothered to follow that through that either. He just wasted his talent. I'd done my best to help him but after that I gave up on him.

After Lilac Time finished I only saw Joe once more and that was a disaster. He was appearing in Plain and Fancy, a new musical comedy and he invited me to go with him to an end of show party given by the star Dolores Grey in her apartment near Marble Arch. Foolishly, I accepted. All went well until it was over and we set off in the early hours to get a taxi. As we walked down Oxford Street, he became very abusive and started shouting and pushing me about. I was feeling very distressed but luckily we were quite close to Piccadilly Circus, where two policemen were on duty. They hailed a taxi for me and when Joe made to get in as well, they asked if I wanted him with me. I said definitely not. They held him back as I drove off and that was the last I ever saw of him, though for a while afterwards he kept phoning my digs. I always refused to speak to him but one morning he arrived at my digs and started banging on the door and shouting. I kept quiet and hid away until he finally left and thank heavens he never came back. I heard on the grapevine some years later that he had died from a severe heart attack when he was still quite young. I suppose the drinking must have finally caught up with him.

This time, Lilac Time had a more extended tour planned than the previous productions I'd been in, and included a visit to Ireland. A few weeks into the tour, we were playing in Truro and about to go to the Olympic theatre in Dublin when the leading lady, Peggy Allan, was taken ill and rushed to hospital with a terrible chest infection. After emergency treatment she was moved into a nursing home on steam inhalations, so the company had leave her behind. When she recovered she did follow us to Dublin where she had some friends, but she wasn't fit to sing and had to convalesce for quite a while. It turned out that her misfortune was my blessing.

In Dublin I took over Peggy's role and we did some concerts after the show as well which was very nice. Afterwards we went on to Cork. Every year in Cork they had a two-week International choral festival at the city's Opera House, which was part of wider celebrations called the An Tostal. This festival mainly staged opera and always engaged an orchestra and conductor with professional singers to sing the lead roles accompanied by an amateur operatic chorus. The Australian singers' agent had arranged for the people who ran the Festival to listen to her clients came along to Lilac Time hear these two Australians singing, but of course they heard me instead of Peggy. Afterwards the talent scouts came to my dressing room and asked me if I'd be interested in the part of Flora in La Traviata which they were going to do for the An Tostal. Of course I was interested! Can a fish swim?

They asked me about my experience, so I told them about my singing lessons with Frank Mullings. They wanted to know if I had sung Flora before, but of course I hadn't. I hadn't sung any opera at all apart from the arias Frank Mullings had taught me. One of the men produced a score of La Traviata and asked me to glance through it. I looked at it and said 'Oh yes it'll suit me fine'. it was a mezzo soprano role and I knew it was well within my range. 'I don't know the part but I'll learn it' I promised. They looked at each other and seemed to be hesitating, so I thought quickly and said 'I can sing One Fine Day for you'. One Fine Day goes from a low B flat to a top B, which I could see was the range required for the part of Flora. 'All right', they said. 'We'll hear you after the last show'. So as we were packing up after the show on the last night they appeared again and we all went over to the local pub. At 1 o'clock in the morning in a half empty bar, I sang One Fine Day and that was it. The part of Flora was mine! I was booked to perform in February the following year in the Cork Opera House.

After Lilac Time came back to England and finished its tour I found myself temporarily out of work again. Between stage roles I would apply for all sorts of jobs and shortly after leaving Lilac Time I saw an advert for a job at Locarno ballroom in Streatham which was run by Mecca. I went to see the manager and he gave me a job as an usherette. The manager's name was Eric Morley. He was a young man at that time, just starting to make his way with Mecca. Of course, he did very well subsequently and became well known when he started organising the Miss World contests.

He was a tubby, not very attractive little man when I met him (he got thinner years later after he married Julia). He took quite a shine to me and wined and dined me a few times and actually invited me to move in with him as I had nowhere permanent to stay, but I said 'No thank you very much!'

He wasn't offended by my rejection and fixed me up in digs with his aunt Doris who lived at Thornton Heath, which was quite near to Streatham. I lodged with her often after that and we became good friends. Eric gave me a job with evening shifts so I could attend auditions, which was generous of him considering I'd spurned his advances!

Streatham Locarno was a beautiful ballroom where they staged the national ballroom dancing championships. It was very popular at that time and was always full of dancing couples. Set around the dance floor there were lots of tables. Nearly everyone smoked in those days (though I never did) and every table had an ashtray. Scattered around between the tables were big mushroom-like bins which the waiters used to tip all the ashtrays in when they were full.

One night, soon after I started working there and was taking tickets at the door, two men came in. One was a tall, rather Jewish-looking gentleman, and his friend was a funny little drunken Irishman. It was my job, halfway through the evening to go round and sell a newspaper called 'Dance News' which was all about forthcoming dance championships. I was going round selling these papers—I think they were threepence each—when I came to the table where this tall dark man was sitting, looking very bored, while his little drunken friend jigged around the dance floor with one girl after another, enjoying himself. The tall man's face lit up when I appeared and he started chatting me up. I was a bit of a flirt in those days and we exchanged banter for a minute or two. Eventually I said, 'Well excuse me I've got to sell these papers', and tried to move on. Without warning he lunged at me and took them out of my hand—a big batch of them—and counted them up. 'There you are' he said, and he counted out some money, paid me for the lot and dumped them in the mushroom cigarette bin.

Now, he went on, 'I've bought a little of your time, so talk to me. What's a girl like you doing in as place like this? Blah de blah...'

I thought 'Oh Lord!', but what could I do? I had no more papers to sell so I stayed on and talked to him. He asked if he could take me home when I'd finished my shift, but I was becoming quite skilled at dealing with such passes by now and said. 'Look, no thanks, you've got your hands full with your Irish friend'.

'Well, will you meet me for lunch in the West End then?' he asked. As it happened I used to go to the West End most days when I was off duty to do auditions. And a free lunch was a free lunch! So I said all right.

I met him in a restaurant the next day before auditions started. Over lunch, he told me his name was Rupert Leon, he was divorced and he was in the steel business. I told him that I was trying to get a job in show business-and he said 'Oh, I've got a lot of contacts in show business. I could help you there'. I thought 'I bet you have' I didn't believe a word of it.

'We're having a party tomorrow' he continued.' My friend who was with me at the Locarno yesterday has a mistress who lives in Aylesbury and we're having a little dinner party for both of them with some of his friends before he goes back home to Ireland. Why don't you join us?

The party was being held in one of the top restaurants in London. So I met them at there and found myself seated at a big table with fifteen other people, including this little Irish man who had eyes for nobody but his mistress. The rest of us might as well not have been there! The two of them went off early—he was taking her back to Aylesbury—but the party continued without them. When we finally broke up all the ladies in the group—I think there were about 7 of us—were given a packet of DuPont nylons, which were the first nylons to come out of America. You didn't have nylon stockings before that. I went home and showed Doris, thrilled to bits.

Before I left, Rupert had asked me what I was doing on Saturday afternoon. When I said 'Nothing', he said 'Well, meet me at Hampton Court and I'll get a picnic organised'. So we went to Hampton Court and sat out under the trees on a rug, drank champagne and ate lovely food. Suddenly, without any warning, he leaned towards me said 'Joan I've got a proposition to put to you'.

Uh oh, I thought.

'Oh yes?' I said

'I have a daughter, Julia, who's at school at Roedean. I'm visiting her there next Sunday. If you'd like to come with me, I'll book a double room for us at the Metropole Hotel in Brighton'. Before I had time to digest that suggestion he added 'Look, by now you must know that I really like you Joan, so I've got another proposition. I would like to set you up in a flat in Mayfair. I'll pay for the flat. I'll give you an allowance to buy clothes and I'd' like you to become my mistress and accompany me to Royal Ascot, Henley Regatta, you name it.'

'Oh yes?' I repeated, a bit stunned by how quickly things were moving.

'And don't forget,' he added, as if it would clinch the deal. 'I can help your career with all my contacts in show business'.

I just looked at him and I thought. No, I don't think so. I didn't believe his story, for a moment. And in any case he wasn't my cup of tea at all. He wasn't Irish. He didn't have charm. Rupert must have guessed my reaction by the expression on my face because he held his hand up said that of course he didn't expect an answer right way. He gave me his card and said 'if you decide to accept my proposition, just phone me on this number and I'll pick you up and we'll go to Brighton together'.

I went home and told Doris about it and we had a bit of a laugh before I tore up the card and threw it in the bin. Afterwards, I carried on with my job at the Locarno for a few weeks. but to my relief I never saw Rupert Leon there again.

Years later I was in a dentists waiting room somewhere and browsing through a copy of Tatler, when I saw his face staring out at me. He was wearing an army officer's uniform. Sure enough the caption said Rupert Leon but it also said that he was the former husband of the actress Margaret

Lockwood. She was a huge film star during the '50s who made it big in Hollywood. The article was all about how her career had taken off in the '40s while Rupert was in the army abroad during the war and they had divorced two or three years after his return. So it had been true after all that he had influential contacts in show business. But I didn't regret my decision. Being a kept woman had never been part of my career plan.

Funnily enough I learned years afterwards that Julia, Rupert's daughter with Margaret Lockwood, who Rupert had been going to take me to visit at Roedean, had become a famous actress herself.

After a few weeks at the Locarno, I was offered a job with a few other singers to dub for an ice pantomime of Tom Arnolds called Sleeping Beauty on ice at the Empire theatre in Liverpool. I had to dub for a champion ice skater Jacqueline du Boeuf. I'd be sitting in the orchestra pit in a mediaeval costume doing her singing voice while she mimed. I made it clear when I took the job that I needed to be excused for 3 weeks in February to go to the Cork Festival and the production company was quite agreeable to that.

Liverpool of course was a huge port, so was very handy for boats. I found that I could get a cattle boat from Liverpool straight through to Cork for very little money, so at the beginning of February1954 I booked myself onto it. it was very nice. I sat up in the bar with the crew most of the evening having a drink and playing cards. I had a nice little berth and they even put a hot water bottle in my bed. We sailed into Cork in the early morning so I got to the theatre before all the rest of the cast.

Over Christmas, the Cork festival organisers had rung me up wanting some information about me for the publicity material for their programmes. I didn't know what to say. As

I'd already told them, I hadn't done any opera before, although of course I'd learned a lot of arias while studying with Frank Mullings. But that, and my career in light opera didn't really sound impressive enough, even to me. I was desperate to avoid giving the impression that I was just a lightweight singer who got lucky because the leading lady fell ill. And then, in the nick of time a light went on the back of my mind and I said, more confidently than I felt, 'Of course I am a descendant of the great Simms Reeves'.

It seems I had said exactly the right thing. My supposed relationship with the great man appeared in all the programmes and when I first arrived at the opera house in Cork, a man came up to me. "So you're Joan Booth' he said. 'Come with me!' and he led me to a room right at the back of the opera house with a huge glass dome in the roof. On the wall hung a photograph of a great big moustachioed man. 'Isn't that your ancestor Simms Reeves' he said? I hadn't a clue,' but I bluffed my way through. 'Ooh yes', I said 'It looks a bit like him.'

We had just ten days of rehearsals before the festival. Patricia Baird was singing the lead role of Violetta. She was an Australian soprano who was doing a lot of broadcasting on the BBC at that time with the conductor and presenter Eric Robinson. She had a really great voice but let's just say she had a good face for radio!

I really loved every minute of that adventure in Cork. On the night of the dress rehearsal, all the local VIPs were invited to attend. There was a reception afterwards in the bar and we met all the top people in the town. During the evening I was introduced to one gentleman who looked strangely familiar. He was with his wife, but I didn't recognise her at all. I stared at him, trying to work out were I'd seen him before, and all at once I remembered. 'Oh my God, it's that funny little

Irishman that was drunk in the Locarno' I thought. 'And I know he's got a mistress in Aylesbury!' And here he was with his wife!

He didn't know me from Adam. because I'd never really spoken to him. He'd been drunk and he was completely absorbed with this other woman when I'd met him, so he didn't recognise me, but I certainly recognised him and thought 'Oh gosh. Could I tell a story!' Such a coincidence.

The opera went down a storm and was a sell-out every night with very good reviews. It was all over far too soon and afterwards I had to go back on the cattle boat to rejoin Sleeping Beauty on Ice. This time I had extra luggage. While I was appearing at the Opera House I had my portrait painted by a man called Frank Sanquest. He later became a renowned artist in Ireland and only died in 2007 in his nineties. The painting was enormous but I was determined to carry it home and somehow, with the crew's help, managed to transport it with me all the way back on the boat to Liverpool. It hangs in my sitting room to this day...

After the Ice show closed, I again started looking for jobs which would pay the bills until I found some stage work. One of these jobs was selling Silver Scissors Patterns in Lewis's store in Birmingham. They were dressmaking patterns. I didn't know anything about dressmaking, but I did the spiel and found I was pretty good at selling these things, making quite a few friends in the process. I used to finish work at midday on Saturday, when I'd get on the train and go home to my parents for the weekend.

While I was working at Lewis's, the Covent Garden Opera Company came to Manchester to put on a show. Their conductor, Colin Davis, was auditioning singers as the company toured the country and Frank Mullings encouraged me to apply. I was more than happy to follow his advice, since performing in opera was still my ultimate dream. Colin Davis seemed to like me very much 'We hold the follow up auditions in London in a few months' he told me.' When we are next recruiting singers I'll send for you'. I walked out of the audition room on Cloud Nine!

Soon afterwards, I auditioned for a job in a big review called Startime that was going to open at the Coventry Hippodrome in the summer of 1954. I won the part, which was exciting because it had some big names. It starred the comedians Ben Jewell and Jimmy Warriss. Geraldo's band were on stage and it also had an orchestra in the pit. The female lead was Sally Barnes, a comedian who did impersonations and was quite a big television star. We did all sorts of little sketches in that show. One of the scenes was in a hat shop, where I had to sign invoices and hand hats to Sally Barnes while she did her impersonations. I also performed in a sketch with Jimmy Jewell where he did that Gene Kelly number Singing in the rain and I was holding an umbrella, singing do di do doo do di do doo.

It was fun but not very rewarding from a singing point of view, so it was bad timing that whilst I was doing pop stuff in this revue and not bothering very much about my real singing I finally got the call to go to London for my audition for Covent Garden. My appointment was at 9 am which meant I would have to get up very early to catch the train to London

.

Of course I was thrilled to bits, but I was also very nervous about it. On top of being out of practice, I wasn't very good at auditions. I used to get so uptight that I would tighten up my voice and wouldn't always produce the sound I was capable of. I confided my fears to one of the musicians in Geraldo's band; a Scottish chap, who played the clarinet and the saxophone, and who was also a very good artist-his speciality was drawing birds. I'd become quite friendly with him so I asked him how he coped with nerves.

'Oh you'll be all right,' he reassured me. 'I'll give you something to take when you're on the train'. He gave me two tablets, which I took at 7 am, soon after I caught the train. It was a big mistake. By the time I got to Covent Garden I was like a zombie. I don't know to this day what was in them, but they 'relaxed' me far too much! I auditioned in the big high hallway in Covent Garden but I felt so dazed and confused that I was totally unable to do myself justice. I knew, even before I got the letter confirming it, that I hadn't got through. It was something I regretted for the rest of my life because opera was the one thing that I really wanted to do.

CHAPTER 5

After Startime finished its season at the Coventry Hippodrome it went on tour around the country. I carried on singing in the show but Geraldo and his orchestra didn't join us on tour and so the singing became even less rewarding. In any case, after my disappointment over my Covent Garden audition my heart just wasn't in it.

So it was a relief when, shortly before the end of 1954, I received a call offering me a part in another Leon Underwood production of Lilac Time. This time, I finally I found myself offered the lead role of Lili. I couldn't believe my luck.

Once again a long tour was planned, starting in the spring. Joe Sealy wasn't in the cast of this production, thank goodness, but someone I had never come across before, a New Zealander called Leslie Andrews, was singing the role of Schubert. Leslie was from Timoru and had originally come over to England to study at London's Royal College of Music. Afterwards, he had been asked to sing at Glyndebourne and had decided to stay in England for a while to try his luck. He was a lovely man, rather short with thick waves of sandy hair. Very warm and funny. Apart from his accent, He might almost have been Irish!

In the operetta, as Lili, I played the love of Schubert's life and well before the end of the tour, as often happens on the stage, life had imitated art and we had become an item. Unfortunately for me, Leslie had a wife and two children in London, so I knew our relationship was never going to go anywhere, but I couldn't help myself. As the tour went on I found myself falling for him more and more. It was the start of the first real love affair of my life...

One summer day in 1955, soon after my affair with Leslie began, we were playing in Leeds when a woman turned up at the theatre and asked to speak to Leslie, me and Robert Glynne, the baritone who played Schober. She handed us her card and wasted no time in getting to the point. 'I represent the Eleanor Agency' she said. 'Have you ever thought of singing in the working men's clubs up here in the North?'

We hadn't, but when she told us what we would get paid for doing a short act (or 'turn' as she called it) on a Sunday night in one of the Yorkshire clubs, the idea definitely appealed. It seemed we could earn as much in one day at a club as we did for a week on tour in Lilac time. The three of us worked out that if we sneaked off on Sunday morning *when* the rest of the cast was getting on the train and heading for the next venue, we could fit it in without anybody noticing. We guessed the management wouldn't be too pleased to find out that we were moonlighting, so we agreed not to tell them. Between us we hatched a cunning plan.

All the cast used to be given their train tickets to the next venue with their wages at the end of the week. Every Sunday morning the cast was supposed to get on the train with all their luggage while the backstage people loaded the scenery and costumes on the same train. Like most the others, I had a big trunk which I packed all my things into. The three of us would make sure our luggage was on board, get on the train with the rest of the cast, then sidle through the train and get out again at the other end. After that we'd catch a different train to wherever we were booked to play a club that Sunday. For a couple of months, the trick worked really well, although sometimes we had to change stations two or three times if we were a long way from Yorkshire. We'd arrive at the club and do an afternoon and an evening act. Each of us would do solo spots first and then we'd sing the duets from Lilac Time. Very naughty! We'd stay the Sunday night in digs and travel back by train early the next morning. When we arrived at the next venue on Monday we would join up at the theatre, collect our luggage, which had travelled up with the rest of the cast and carry on as if nothing had happened.

We might have got away till the end of the tour with it but for one thing. We had a stage manager on Lilac Time who had taken a bit of a fancy to me. He kept trying to make up to me and make dates. I had always cold-shouldered him. I couldn't stand the little man. But of course, because he was keeping an eye on me, he started to notice that I was going off with these two men every Sunday and that we were missing our train calls. He didn't realise what we were really doing and I'm sure he thought I was up to no good with Leslie and Robert and was jealous. That seems the only explanation for what happened next.

It all kicked off when we were about to play the Dudley Hippodrome near Birmingham. I had got to know a lot of people in Birmingham while I was working there selling dress patterns and I had kept in touch with them and told them I was playing the lead role in Lilac Time, so when we opened at Dudley, many of them had promised to come and see me in the show.

As luck would have it, I was late getting to the theatre on the opening night because I'd been doing one of these gigs the day before. The Hippodrome was a lovely big theatre, with three large dressing rooms close to the stage for the principals, When I ran into the theatre, completely out of breath and opened the door to the dressing room I should have been in, I found to my shock that the man who paid the wages was using it as his office. In the second big dressing room, the manager had put the two girls who played the minor sisters' roles. In the third, he'd put Leslie and Robert Glynne. When I eventually found the door which had my name on, it was in a row of little rabbit hutches way down the corridor which were meant for the chorus. It was ridiculous. Lili was a very big part and I was on the stage nearly all the time so I needed to be near the stage, not stuck down a corridor.

I went up to the stage manager and played hell. 'What do you think you're playing at, putting me in that little shoebox?'

He just shrugged. 'Well it's your own fault. You weren't on the train call to collect your tickets on Sunday morning. For all we knew you weren't going to turn up'. Furious, I ran into to Robert and Leslie 's dressing room 'Have you seen where they've put me?' I asked. 'And I 've got friends coming to see me tonight. What on earth are they going to think? This isn't on'.

Leslie and Robert were as angry as I was and kicked up a big stink about it. 'We'll go on strike' they announced. They went to the theatre managers, the Kennedy brothers, and told them 'We're not going on unless you give Joan a proper dressing room'.

That put the cat among the pigeons. Everybody was rushing about like mad trying to decide what to do. Nobody wanted to move out of the rooms they'd been given, but I was really on my high horse by now. 'I'll tell you what' I said to the boys. 'If they won't move, I'll move in with you'. So I took all my stuff into Robert and Leslie's dressing room.

Well, the show went on of course., but the whole management was furious and threatened to black ball me. By the time I went on stage I was nearly in tears (the show went particularly well that night because I was so emotional!)

Unknown to me, my move into the men's dressing room had done the trick. During the interval I found that they had moved the manager out of his unofficial office and put me back in there instead. It meant that after the show I was able to entertain my friends in the Number One dressing room after all. But I was in trouble with the management for quite a while!

A month or two later the Lilac Time tour finished and Leslie and I had to look for more work. We weren't able to find work together as we'd hoped but agreed to stay in touch.

For my next job I found myself a role as principal boy in a touring version of the pantomime Little Bo Peep. I don't remember much about it except that Ted Lune, the comedian was in it and we opened at Hulme Hippodrome, and finished up in Bolton.

While I did Bo Peep, Leslie was dubbing for another Pantomime on Ice with Norman Wisdom at the Empress Hall Earls Court. He was able to get away one weekend to see me perform Bo Peep, but our meetings were forced to be few and far between.

One quite exciting event to happen that winter was that I appeared on television for the first time. My old singing teacher, Frank Cummings had recently died and his wife had started an agency with a Granada TV producer. That year ATV were running a TV talent show called Bid for Fame and I was asked to appear on it. Alan Ferguson had written a song called Good Morning Mrs Jones, which they asked me to perform this with the Joe Loss Band and a Canadian crooner-type singer. The song was a bit stupid really. I started off wearing a coat and hat and I was supposed to be Mrs Jones—then this Canadian man appeared singing 'Good morning Mrs Jones and how's your beautiful daughter' and the next minute everything was whipped off me and I was sitting in a negligee in front of a dressing table singing 'la di lah di lah' before going into a song and dance act as the daughter! They televised it live on a Sunday when the panto wasn't on. I thought it was all completely daft, but they must have thought it was all right because they brought me back for the second round of the competition and I was summoned to Harrogate in the spring of 1956 for the next show.

This time, they wanted some of the songs I'd been singing in the pantomime, which weren't really my cup of tea-I think I did one of those Frank Sinatra numbers-but it went out on TV again and I got some write-ups in the local paper and a rather glamorous photo of me as the principal boy in Little Bo Peep...

In 1956 I got a summer season engagement at the Opera House in St Helier. Leslie tried to find work in Jersey with me, but they already had a tenor in the show and he ended up appearing in Star Wagon with Sandy Powell at the Royal Hippodrome Eastbourne.

There were some quite good acts appearing with me at the Opera house, including the comedian Peter Doulay. There was also a double act; Ken Morris and Joan Savage. Ken played the piano while Joan sang and did impersonations. It was quite a good little set-up. We did different programmes every week.

I loved Jersey. I got digs with a nice Scottish lady in a very lovely modern house a mile or so out of St Helier, a few strides from the beach. I hired a bicycle and after sunbathing all day I used to ride back and forwards to the theatre on this bike. I loved my first experience of Jersey and after that I always wanted to go back there. You got a decent wage which kept the wolf from the door. Of course, you never earned a fortune in musical theatre unless you were a star.

When the summer came to an end I did a pantomime season at the Palace Theatre Plymouth which was staging Puss in Boots. Leslie was able to get work with me at last, playing Crispin the old cobbler. I was cast as the Fairy Queen who turns Puss's footwear into magic boots, although I hated being a fairy. It just wasn't me!

After the pantomime, Leslie and I were able to find yet another job together; this time in London, in the Lyons corner house near Marble Arch. The Corner House had several restaurants at different levels. The basement restaurant, called the Quebec, was one of the largest restaurants in London and it was here that we performed twice a day. Joseph Hoffer and his Viennese ensemble were the main attraction and Leslie and I were employed to sing with the band, doing solos and duets. It was a really good job for us. We used to go to the Cumberland hotel next door, where we had a little dressing room in there, and get into our Viennese costumes. I wore a Tyrolean dirndl and embroidered blouse and Leslie was in leather trousers and a little hat with a feather. Then we'd walk back together through a little tunnel leading from the Cumberland kitchens into the Quebec Rooms and join the band on stage. We didn't sing any great music. It was mainly little pop songs of the day, first individually, then together, putting harmonies to them. We used to get terrific appreciative audiences, particularly for afternoon teas. Afterwards, we'd go back through the tunnel to the hotel before appearing again for dinner in the evenings. It was a great job. At the weekends we'd set off together on the train to Yorkshire and do a club, so we ended up earning quite good money.

On top of this, we kept getting little surprise jobs on the side. One day a little old lady came up to me at the Corner House and told me she's written a song which she wanted me to record for her in a studio. It wasn't a very good song but I was paid, so I didn't argue!

Another night, a man called Alfredo came in who was a gypsy violinist with an orchestra which he was taking around all the big exhibitions. He wanted a singer for this orchestra and after he heard me sing in the Quebec room he booked me to do three shows with them the following year.

When the Quebec rooms engagement came to an end, Leslie and I carried on doing the clubs at weekends while we both looked for other work.

One day I saw an advert in The Stage for people to teach ballroom dancing and because I'd had dancing lessons and could dance reasonably well, I decided to apply for it. So did dozens of others. At the audition I picked up what they wanted me to do very quickly compared with some of the applicants, so I was picked out and offered me a job at the London Dance Institute in Oxford Street. It wasn't a big flashy place. You had to go downstairs to the basement just to find it. People went there not so much to meet up and socialise but to learn proper ballroom dancing. To start with I would just sell dances. I'd have a quarter of an hour with one person and then have a break. Then I'd dance with someone else. But my real job was to chat the punters up and sell them courses of lessons leading towards a medal qualification. I'd say 'You know you're nearly ready for your bronze now'. And that would mean a tuition package that would cost them a few hundred pounds. They'd sign up for this and then you'd have to take them up to standard to get their bronze medal.

You got a basic wage but there was a commission at the end of the year for the person who sold the most dance sessions. I found it very hard work though, because I was there all day from morning to night, having beginners treading on my toes and being on my feet for hours on end.

But exhausting as it was, there were some funny moments. I had one pupil, a very tall thin Indian man who always wore white gloves. I think maybe his religion meant he wasn't supposed to come into close contact with women and that was why he wore these gloves all the time. He was a surgeon at one of the London hospitals but he couldn't dance for the life of him. He hadn't an ounce of rhythm in his body. He was like a big unbendable stick and I used to have to push him around. I'd think to myself 'you'll never pass a dancing exam in your life'. But for some reason, he kept on coming for lessons…

And then there was another American guy who was nice. He was an airline pilot with quite an important job at some big airport in America and he met a lot of important people and was sometimes expected to dance with the ladies. He picked it up quickly. I didn't sign him up for any exams because he was going back to America quite soon. One day he invited me out to lunch. You weren't supposed to fraternise with your pupils, but as he was going back I thought it would be all right, so I accepted and we had a good time. He was quite a jolly chap.

I missed singing, so I grabbed every chance I had to keep in practice. After I'd finished teaching at the Institute I would sometimes go for a meal to a big Chinese restaurant in Soho. They employed a Greek singer and his group to entertain the diners and I was quick to introduce myself to them. Soon, I was singing a duet with the singer every night when I'd finished my meal!

Leslie was still in London, but like me, he was struggling to get much singing work. One day he came to see me and told me that his little girl had been very ill with a chest problem and his wife wanted to go back to New Zealand.

'The doctors have told us that the New Zealand climate would be better for her' he said. 'So for the sake of my child I'd better go.' It was hard news to take. We had sung such a lot together and we were a good team.

I don't think Leslie's marriage was particularly successful. He'd met his wife at college when they were both learning to sing, and I think there was always a problem when he got on well in his career and she didn't. He had tried to get her singing with him in shows but they usually rejected her, so she mustn't have been as good as he was. Of course, that had led to a bit of friction because she was always envious of him and he was always going off to perform. But anyway I never asked him or expected him to abandon his wife and his three children. I always knew it wasn't going to go anywhere, but I was very, very fond of him. I think if he'd been free we'd probably have married. But I knew the score from the word go, so even though I was quite upset, I wasn't surprised. It had to be.

So off Leslie went to New Zealand. He had nothing planned. He was heading for Auckland. He wrote to me just once to tell me he had no work and was working on the docks just to make ends meet. Afterwards he did get back into show business in quite a big way, but it was to be many years later, when I was happily married myself, before I learned all about that!

CHAPTER 6

After Leslie left for New Zealand in 1957, I went home for Christmas. I had crowned my spell at the Dance Institute by winning the end of year cash prize for selling the most dances. They were keen for me to go back in the New Year, but I was completely fed up with it. 'Honestly, I can't go back to that' I told my parents. 'It's killing me. My feet are ruined …' The other teachers used to tell me to plunge my feet into cold water and then plunge them into hot water every evening, but I couldn't be doing with it any more. It was soul destroying. With few regrets, I wrote and resigned.

At this time of my life I used to stay with my parents quite a lot. They had been struggling to make the pub pay, so they had given up the tenancy and were now living in Cale Green, Stockport. Mother was working as a shop assistant in Cheadle and Dad had become a driving instructor at my Uncle Abe's driving school in Stockport.

It was too late to apply for a part in panto, so I didn't do anything that Christmas and just took it easy at home. I did have a couple of singing lessons though. Since my singing teacher, Frank Mullings had died, his accompanist Fay Seaston had taken over his pupils and whenever I was at home I would go over to her studio and have a little session with her—we'd become good friends. Once, a year or so before, I had arrived for a lesson while Fay was teaching a businessman called Stanley Ross, and she had introduced us to each other.

Stanley owned a factory in Manchester that made ladies coats. He had dark brown hair and wasn't bad looking. He had tried to chat me up that first time we met, but I was involved with Leslie then and wasn't interested. He had stayed keen on me however, and since then we had met up for a meal once or twice and he used to come and visit me whenever I was appearing near Manchester. That Christmas he got in touch again and we went out together on a few dates. It wasn't a great love affair or anything like that. I didn't even find Stanley particularly attractive, but he was good company. I was at a loose end and trying to get over Leslie, so he filled a gap.

In the New Year I went back to London because I had seen a general audition advertised in The Stage for the West End production of My Fair Lady. The show had recently been a huge hit on Broadway and I was really keen to get into the chorus. On the first audition there were hundreds of other hopefuls but I got through with my singing, and felt quite optimistic. The second audition was before a panel where I had to sing again. Once again, I felt it went quite well. Afterwards the panel started asking me questions about my previous experience. I had just launched into an account of my career so far, when one of the men interrupted me. 'Excuse me, Miss Booth. You seem to have a Lancashire accent' he said. 'Well, yes, I am from Manchester' I answered. And that was it. It was hello and goodbye. They only wanted Londoners. They didn't even give me a chance to show them I *could* do a Cockney accent.

That same week I auditioned for another show—a new musical called Gentleman's Pastime and got a part in the chorus. Once again, it wasn't my type of music, but it was a job. Gentleman's Pastime was written and produced by a woman called Ma Pastime was written and produced by a woman called Marion Hart, who was married to Richard Adler, the composer of The Pajama Game, another big hit musical of the time. It was being put on at the Players Theatre, which was a small theatre in Charing Cross with a little restaurant attached to it. 'The Players' operated mainly as an Edwardian style music hall (Leonard Sachs was the be-whiskered compere who became quite famous playing the same role in the TV show 'The Good Old Days'), but from time to time it also used to put on musicals. A few years earlier, 'The Boyfriend' which later became a West End hit with Julie Andrews, had opened there. I think Marion Hart's dream was that Gentleman's Pastime would follow suit. Marion Hart was a very glamorous lady, who looked a bit like a young Ava Gardner, but she turned out to be rather temperamental and difficult to work with.

One of the stars of the show was a well-known singer called Janet Hamilton Smith, who played the part of the housekeeper. She was famous for doing a double act with her husband John Hargreaves. They were rather like Anne Ziegler and Webster Booth, singing light opera and Ivor Novello stuff and they also did quite a lot of radio. One of the songs Jane had to sing in Gentleman's Pastime was a proper operatic number, so although I was in the chorus, I was really brought in to understudy her, which was quite a prestigious booking.

The musical was a bit like My Fair Lady, but instead of the female Eliza Doolittle character learning to be a lady it was all about thieves being trained to be gentlemen. My Fair Lady, of course, went on to be a big success, but unfortunately the same couldn't be said for Gentleman's Pastime. It was quite a good romantic story but one of the songs was an absolute steal from Marion Hart's husband's show The Pajama Game. As soon as I heard the intro to this song I thought—Hello. I know this. I nearly went into 'Hey there, you with the stars in your eyes… '

Not surprisingly, when it opened in March the critics straight away picked up the similarity with the My Fair Lady storyline as well as the stolen song and they panned it. It finished its month's run at the Players Theatre, but it never did transfer to the West End.

Since I'd first met him, while performing in Dick Whittington in Chorlton, I'd become good friends with the composer Alan Ferguson, and one evening he came to see me perform in Gentleman's Pastime, bringing with him Harry H Corbett, who I'd not met since our season together in pantomime. In the meantime, Harry had become a respected Shakespearean actor, working with Joan Littlewood's Theatre Workshop. In one theatre review he had been described as 'The English Marlon Brando'. Nobody then would have guessed that his serious acting was to fall by the wayside a few years later when he became world famous for his role in the hit TV comedy Steptoe and Son.

After the show, the three of us had dinner together in the theatre restaurant. During the meal Alan Ferguson invited me to the Tin Pan Alley Ball at the Dorchester hotel a week or so later, for which he was composing some music. Of course, I accepted immediately.

It was a really interesting evening with lots of show business singing stars and soon-to-be stars present. I remember seeing one very handsome young man jiving the night away with a woman who I recognized as Dorothy Squires, the pop singer. She had recently had a big hit with a song called The Gypsy, which had been written by her first husband, the composer Billie Reid. The couple had been notorious for their partying. Show business gossip told of dozens of empty bottles left behind in the dressing room of every show they performed in.

Alan told me that the handsome young man dancing with Dorothy Squires that night was the actor Roger Moore, who was now Dorothy's second husband. At that time, Dorothy Squires was much more famous than Roger Moore, who was 13 years her junior. The show business gossip was that he had married her to get more work—it was a way for him to step up the ladder. If that was true, it certainly paid off. A year or two after that Tin Pan Alley Ball, Roger Moore became famous as Simon Templar, the star of The Saint, a long running TV series which in turn led to his casting as Agent 007 in several of the James Bond films of the seventies.

There were a lot of people from the pop world at the Ball (among them Matt Munro (little did I know then that I would sing with him in a few years' time). Alan seemed to know most of them. 'Do you see that girl over there?' he said, pointing to a tall, rather gawky coloured girl on the far side of the room. 'She's going to be one of the most famous people here in a few months.'

I wasn't particularly impressed. 'She looks very plain. What's her name? 'I asked.

'Shirley Bassey.' Alan said. I'd never heard of her, but Alan was right. They were about to release her big time into the pop world. Six months later, in January 1959 she had her first number one hit 'As I love you' I and after that her career never looked back. She didn't look glamorous at all, the night I saw her. Her clothes were ordinary and she looked very angular with awful hair. But when she was on stage she was transformed. I think she wore wigs to perform later on. She was a great artiste with a unique and amazing voice and in the years that followed I became a great fan of hers.

Since Christmas, Stanley Ross had made a point of calling me on the phone whenever he'd been in London on business and we had met up and had several meals out together. When Gentleman's Pastime finished, he rang again and told me he was going on holiday to the South of France for two weeks and asked if I'd like to go with him? Ever up for an adventure, I naturally said yes.

We drove through France in Stanley's Jaguar, stopping somewhere midway overnight before going on to a lovely villa that he'd booked outside Monte Carlo. It was very nice break. We went to the casino in Monte Carlo and saw firework displays and parades in Nice. One night, we went for dinner to the Hotel Negresco, which was very grand. A chap called Robin Douglas-Hume was playing the piano there, and Stanley told me he was a nephew of the British prime minister Alex Douglas-Hume.

It was the night of the Nuit Blanc, which was similar to the famous Battle of flowers in Jersey, except that all the flowers were white. After dinner we sat on the Promenade des Anglais to watch the parade go by while people threw white flowers off the floats into the crowd. It was spectacular, a lovely evening. I was wearing a dress with a cowl shaped neckline and afterwards when I went to the fancy loo in the Hotel Negresco I discovered that my dress cowl was full of white petals. I had to strip off in the loo to get rid of them all!

Not surprisingly, with all the wining and dining, that was the trip when Stanley and I finally became an item. During the second week of our holiday we moved to a different villa in Roquebrun on the other side of Monte Carlo. There were two apartments in the villa and to his horror Stanley discovered that a married couple he knew quite well from Didsbury near Manchester were staying in the other apartment. It rather shook him. He seemed terribly embarrassed. Though he was a bachelor, so I couldn't understand why...

After we came back from France I started auditioning again. One day, an agent rang me and said 'Ivy Benson is looking for a singer for the summer season in the Isle of Man. She wants someone with a trained voice able to sing ballads. Can you meet her for an audition?'

Of course I could! Everybody had heard of Ivy Benson and her all girl band. They played mainly swing songs and had become very popular in the fifties.

I met Ivy Benson in a recording studio in North London. She was middle aged, blonde and very friendly. We got on like a house on fire. Do you know 'I've got a handful of songs to sing you?' she asked. She handed me several sheets of music and accompanied me as I sang several songs in different styles. She was very nice and complimentary and seemed more than happy with me.

'Would you like to join us at the Villa Marina in the Isle of Man for the season?' she asked. Delighted, I said yes.

Suddenly, she seemed to have an afterthought 'By the way, we're doing a Sunday concert at the Odeon in Llandudno in a week's time 'she said. 'Can you come and sing a couple of solo spots with us?'

I agreed to that too and a week later Stanley drove me over to Wales in his big Jag.

Ivy Benson met us as we walked into the cinema and gave Stanley a long once over before turning to me.

'What are you going to sing?' she asked. I told her 'One Fine day' and 'This is my beloved' from Borodin's Kismet and she nodded. For some reason I thought she seemed cooler towards me than on our previous meeting.

Ivy herself accompanied me on the piano as I sang One Fine Day. It got a terrific reception and I had to take several bows and gestured towards Ivy to make sure she got her share of the applause too. During the interval I was in the dressing room changing my dress for my second spot when one of the girls came in and said 'Miss Benson wants to see you in her dressing room now'.

I went down to see her expecting to be praised for the reception One Fine Day had received. but instead she tore me apart. She criticized my performance and my singing and said she wouldn't be taking me to the Isle of Man after all. I was stunned. And I still had to go on and do my second spot!

Somehow I stumbled through 'This is my Beloved' and left the cinema with Stanley with my confidence well and truly dashed. I was mystified. It seemed so unfair. In the end, Ivy Benson never paid me, so she got a free performance out of me. Maybe that was the point. I didn't bother chasing her about it because I didn't have a contract, so I didn't have a leg to stand on.

After that fiasco I took various small jobs for the summer. I was booked to do three summer exhibitions with the orchestra of Alfredo, the gypsy violinist who had first approached me about working with him at the Quebec Rooms the year before. One of these was in the Kings Hall in Belfast, one in a big hall in Edinburgh, and one in Birmingham. There were a lot of these big exhibitions in the fifties. They went on for three or four days with people advertising food and other merchandise and there was always background entertainment. The shows I took part in had dancing water to music, followed by a fashion parade and then a session with me singing with Alfredo and the orchestra. The Greek singer I used to sing duets with in the Chinese restaurant in Soho was also part of the entertainment. Being a singer in those days meant you lived in quite a small world.

The only other work I was able to find found that summer was in concerts in some of the London Parks and in Lincoln's Inn Fields with Medvodef and his Balalaika Orchestra and Russian dancers. I sang Kalinka while they did a Cossack dance. Variety was the spice of life!

Both the exhibitions and the London work was quite well paid, but I always had to think ahead. The intervals between jobs were sometimes quite long and I had to be careful with money in order to tide me over the gaps. I was still living in digs with Doris in Thornton Heath for which she charged me a very fair rate. Living and travelling in London however was still expensive.

So it was quite a relief when out of the blue, the Eleanor agency got in touch with me. They said they had liked my work so much the last time I'd worked for them that they wanted me to do the Northern club circuit for them again that autumn. They were offering me eight weeks work in hotels, pubs, and clubs. I had really enjoyed playing the clubs with Leslie and Robert Glynne so I accepted straight away. Little did I know that the decision would lead to me meeting my future husband!

One of the first places I performed at that autumn was a hotel called the Duke of Edinburgh in Oldham. I hadn't yet passed my driving test, so Stanley drove me up to Oldham in his Jaguar and dropped me off at the hotel. The Duke of Edinburgh was a big commercial concern owned by a brewery called John Willie Lees who'd recently spent a lot of money giving it a big face lift. They'd opened a big long bar called the Melody bar with a stage at the end and they'd employed a resident lady organist to accompany the artists who were performing. In an adjoining room they'd also opened a very fancy little cocktail bar for residents which did a great trade out of hours.

The very first person I saw when I walked into the hotel was a short chubby broth of an Irish boy, with a wide smile, black curly hair and wearing a monkey jacket. He came over to welcome me and introduced himself as Frank Campbell. He told me he had come over from Galway to shake cocktails at the bar. He was very funny and he made me laugh from the word go. He used to tease me about air pollution in North of England. He claimed he'd arrived in Oldham in the middle of a snowstorm 'I'd never seen black snow before' he said straight-faced.

He was a member of the UK Bar Tenders Guild, which meant he was an expert at mixing everything from dry Martinis to flaming Sambucas. My weak spot for Irishman was instantly rekindled and he seemed to take quite a shine to me too. While I was performing in Oldham, we used to go to the cinema together in the afternoons. Frank also taught me to play poker. On an evening, after I'd sung, I used to sit in the cocktail bar and have a drink and chat to him some more.

The managers of the Duke of Edinburgh, Mr and Mrs Whitaker, had been booking singers every week since the hotel reopened. Up until I appeared there they had all been pop artists—they'd had Jackie Trent for a week before me. So I knew what was required and I tried to sing pop and lighter stuff. Then one night, it was getting late and I'd run out of my repertoire of suitable songs. I was never one to dry up on stage so I thought 'Oh to hell with it' and started to sing some operatic arias.

Singing 'Oh my beloved father' in tights and leotard made quite an impression! Mrs. Whitaker called everyone in from the cocktail bar to hear me 'Eeh have you heard this?' she exclaimed 'That Joan Booth, she's singing opera!' All the punters crammed into the doorway and were all standing gaping and looking at each other in disbelief, saying 'What's this?' It brought the place down and everybody wanted more. So after that I changed into a dress every evening at the end of my spot and sang some decent stuff.

One night, after I'd finished performing, I was sitting in the cocktail bar and happened to pick up a magazine that Frank had behind the bar—it was something to do with the bar trade. I was leafing through this while having a drink and noticed there was a place in Jersey advertising for a cocktail barmaid the following year. 'Oh I'd love to go back to Jersey' I thought. So I wrote a letter applying for this job. Of course they wanted a reference. I hadn't a clue who to put down as a referee, and in the end I gave the name of someone called Don Moore, who I'd got to know vaguely in Jersey on my first trip when he had taken a friend of mine out.

They also wanted to know about my bar tending experience. Well, I had none really, but I told them that I had lived in a pub when I was a child. They obviously weren't impressed because they wrote back and said they were sorry but they wanted someone with more experience than that! So that was that. I forgot all about it.

For the rest of the year as I moved around the clubs, Frank would hire a car on his day off and drive over to Yorkshire to take me out to lunch. He and I became very good friends but at that stage it was no more than that. I didn't really take him seriously. I was four years older than him and besides I was in no mood for settling down. I was having far too much fun!

CHAPTER 7

In 1959 I found myself working at Pontins for the holiday season. Pontins holiday camps had started after the war, about ten years after the first Butlins holiday camp opened, and the two companies were great rivals. Pontins was seen then as bit of poor relation because the entertainment side of things let them down. Where Butlins had redcoats doing concerts, Pontins had nothing. Recently however, they had been advertising for entertainers (later they were called Bluecoats). On the spur of the moment I applied and they gave me a position at the Pontins camp in Paignton for the summer.

Over winter I'd been having driving lessons with my Uncle Abe and had bought myself a little Ford Popular. Whenever I drove to the clubs I would put my L plates on and he'd sit in the passenger seat as my qualified supervisor. Uncle Abe used to like a night out at the clubs so it worked for both of us, though I have to confess that when he couldn't accompany me I just used to put the L plates under my seat and drive across the moors on my own. It wasn't that much different to driving with my Uncle Abe because he was a devil and used to fall asleep in the passenger seat half the time.

I took my first driving test in Rotherham. It was the only time I had ever driven in a big city and I didn't know Rotherham at all, so it was a bad mistake. Halfway through the test I found myself heading the wrong way down a one-way street.

'My advice to you Miss Booth is to apply again for your test straight away' the examiner said as he handed me my fail notice. But next time I suggest you go and suss out the town first!'

That put an end to my plans of driving down to Paignton on my own. So the week after my test my mother drove down to Devon with me and then travelled back home on the train.

The holiday season at the Paignton camp opened with a Sunday concert, which was fine as I was the star of the show, because there was nobody much else performing!

Pontins had been started by Fred Pontin. Paignton, however, which had opened fairly recently, was being run by his brother Len. Len didn't seem to have really thought their entertainment programme through, and after that first concert I discovered there wasn't much for me to do during the week. The management was desperately casting around for ideas. One day they said 'Would you mind being in charge of a children's party with jelly and ice-cream?' I said all right, although I felt a bit nervous as I'd had nothing much to do with children, apart from seeing them across the footlights in panto. I remember during the party one little boy wanted to go to the loo so I took him to the toilet but once we got there I was flummoxed. I thought 'Now what do I do with him? Do I stand him up and tip him over?' I had no idea. Looking after children wasn't my cup of tea at all and I didn't think much of it.

The next thing they asked me to do was to take some of the punters for rounders, so once again I agreed. From my first week I used to organize a rounders game on the lawn nearly every day. It wasn't my idea of fun either but it was lovely sunny weather and I wore shorts all the time and became very brown, so at least it was better than the children's parties.

Because I had quite a lot of spare time I decided to take my driving test again. I didn't follow the examiner's advice about sussing out the town, which was a mistake, my test took place on market day with people and cattle all over the place. Somehow I found my way around without hitting a cow or going down a one-way street and at the end of the test, to my relief the examiner handed me a pass certificate.

Soon afterwards, the great Fred Pontin himself came to Paignton and took me out to a nice country club nearby for a drink. As he was driving me back to the camp he said 'I hear you've just passed your driving test. A friend of mine is coming down here for a week. Would you mind driving him around to do a bit of sightseeing?'

So I ended up taking Fred Pontin's friend around in my little car and accompanying him to all the nearby tourist attractions. He was a bit of a bore, but that was that. I added chauffeur and companion to my list of skills!

In June that year, on Derby day, they had a big sweepstake in the camp and I drew a horse. In those days I didn't know anything about horse racing and I'd never even heard of any of the runners. That afternoon, we went out to the lawn area to play rounders as usual. I organized the punters into teams and started them playing, then I lay on the grass sunbathing with my little portable radio. One of the punters sat down on the grass beside me and started chatting. When I told him I'd drawn a horse, he said 'Well, the Derby's on the radio. Why don't you listen to it? So I tuned it in to the right programme and had the commentary playing. I couldn't make head or tail of what was happening. There was so much shouting and screaming. At the end I didn't even know who'd won. The punter who was listening with me said "What's the name of your horse?' I said 'It's called Parthia'. 'Oh' he said 'You've won the sweepstake. Parthia's won!"

I was thrilled. The prize wasn't a lot, but it would still be welcome, as Pontins were far from generous with their wages.

Every night we ate in a great big hall and Len Pontin, with his wife and all the top brass sat on the top table facing us. For some reason, Mrs. Pontin didn't like me at all. She used to frown whenever she saw me. Anyway, when they announced that the winner of the sweepstake was Parthia I jumped up and I had to walk around to the front, still in my short shorts, to claim my prize from Len Pontin. His little fat wife was sat next to him and as I went up to him I heard her say 'Thank goodness she's won the prize. Perhaps now she'll buy herself a decent pair of shorts!'. I thought 'You cow!'

The next day I was called to the office. 'Mrs Pontin doesn't think you have enough to do 'the manager said 'So we've decided to open a shop and we'd like you to run the shop'.

So I said 'Oh would you? Well I don't think so!' and I refused point blank. 'No! I'm not a shop keeper. This wasn't in my contract,' I told him. 'It's not my fault that you haven't got enough concerts going. You want to get your act together'.

When Mrs Pontin was told that I'd refused, that was it. I was called to the office again and this time Len Pontin was there, looking very embarrassed. 'I'm awfully sorry Joan, but since we haven't enough work for you, we're going to have to let you go' he said. I knew that Len quite liked me so I had no doubt who was behind this.

What happened next was unbelievably well timed. As I was sitting in the office, being given the sack, the phone rang. Len answered it and said. 'Oh it's for you Joan'. I took the receiver from him' Hello?'

"Hello Joan' a man's voice answered. 'It's Charlie Sharpe here from Le Couperon in Rozel. You applied for a job as a cocktail bar waitress with us.

I suddenly remembered the ad in Frank's magazine. Yes, I did, about six months ago I said, 'Well' Mr. Sharpe said 'We employed someone, but she didn't turn out to be suitable so we have taken up your reference. 'he laughed 'The man you gave as a referee Don Moore, said 'well I don't know about her abilities as a cocktail waitress but she's a very charming girl and I'm sure she'd be an asset. '

Charlie Sharpe paused. 'So we'd like you to come over if you're still free. When can you start?'

'Next week?' I asked.

'Great', he said, 'we'll see you then' and he hung up

All this while Len Pontin was sitting there, having just told me I was sacked. I smiled sweetly at him. 'Mr Pontin, will you get my cards ready? I'm off to Jersey now. I've just been offered a job'. He looked stunned—he didn't know it was a bar job of course, and I certainly wasn't going to tell him!

He leaned across the desk towards me 'Will you be on the island at Christmas?' he asked. 'I don't know if I will or not Mr Pontin' I said, puzzled.

He gave me a wheedling smile 'If you are, would you come and do cabaret for us in our hotel in Jersey?"

I had forgotten that Pontin's had a hotel in Jersey. I bet your wife won't like that, I thought. But before I left Len's office, I had agreed to do the Christmas season at The Ritz in St Helier.

The next day I drove back home. Because I had only just passed my test, I hadn't a clue how to look after a car. I was almost home when I realised I was nearly out of petrol. There was no sign of a garage, but I spotted a pub with a little petrol pump beside it, so I went in and walked up to the bar. 'I've driven all the way from Paignton and I've no petrol left in the tank. Could you possibly just top me up?'

The landlord smiled 'Come on love' he said. Out we went and he topped me up and then he took a look under the bonnet and said 'Good God, you're nearly out of oil too'. So he topped me up with oil and thanks to my good Samaritan I managed to get home.

Before I'd set off I'd rung Frank, who by now was working in the Alma Lodge Hotel in Stockport. 'Frank, you'll never believe it. I've got a job at this cocktail bar' I told him. Frank said he'd come and see me off at the airport. In those days the 'departure lounge' at Manchester airport was a little Nissen hut with a bench that you put your luggage on. It wasn't the big airport that it is today. but they did have a little bar. As we sat at the bar waiting for my plane Frank gave me a crash course in mixing cocktails!

Le Couperon on Rozel Bay was absolutely lovely, with a castellated wall separating it from the beach and a little fishing pier where the boats would bring in fresh fish and lobsters each morning. Later on, the Swiss chef would turn them into cordon bleu dishes for the guests.

I was given a very comfortable room in the staff quarters. The owner, Charlie Sharpe had been in a market business in Leeds, but he and his wife had sold up and had put their money into developing Le Couperon as a top class hotel. Between growing up in the bar trade and Frank's lesson I had learned more than enough to get by as a cocktail waitress. One of the members of the local aristocracy, Lady Alderley, was a regular at Le Couperon and she liked a dry martini. I would put ice in the shaker and plenty of gin and not much vermouth and she used to say to her companion in her plummy voice 'That girl (nodding towards me) makes the best martinis on the island' And it was nearly all gin!

Charlie Sharpe was still a market trader at heart. He used to buy in cheap gin and once I caught him filling up empty Gordon's bottles with this other stuff. He quickly put the bottles down and I looked the other way but he knew I'd seen what he was up to. He was a bit of a ladies' man too. He had an attractive wife and three kids. But that didn't stop him making a pass at me whenever he saw a chance!

For me it was the perfect life. I had plenty of time off and was able to sunbathe and swim nearly every day. Then, as the hotel filled up with more customers during July and August. I started doing a bit of singing in the bar. I used to sing French songs Le Fiacre and Sous le Pont de Paris and finish off with the Trish Trasch Polka which went down well because of Jersey's French connections. A lot of the local people still spoke a kind of patois.

Finally, the summer season came to an end, and in September I said a sad goodbye to Le Couperon.

Afterwards, with nothing else in the offing, I signed a contract to perform again for a few weeks in the Northern clubs. Once more, Frank drove over regularly from Oldham to Yorkshire on his days off to take me out. Frank was making it crystal clear that he had fallen for me and that Autumn he followed me all over the place. We'd meet up on our days off, go out to dinner together and on the way back to my digs sometimes we'd stop in the hills and have a little cuddle and canoodle in his car, but that was as far as it went.

I thought Frank was very funny and he was great company, but although I was nearly 30 now I still had no thoughts of settling down for a while yet!

That Christmas 1959 I was offered a role as a pantomime principal boy once more. This time the pantomime was Little Red Riding Hood in the Theatre Royal in Bolton. I played the star role of Robin Hood and was described in the programme as 'Joan Booth, the renowned Principal Boy'! It was too good an offer to turn down so I wrote to Len Pontin and told him I wouldn't be playing at the Ritz in Jersey after all. I didn't feel too bad about letting him down after the way they'd treated me that summer!

In the pantomime I played Robin Hood (though what he had to do with Little Red Riding Hood I don't know). Little Jimmy Clitheroe from the radio show The Clitheroe Kid was also in it. He used to make me laugh. He was a funny little man. A little misery guts offstage, but on stage he was hilarious. There was also a dapper, rather camp young man called John Normington who always used to wear a fancy bow tie. He was playing the Big Bad Wolf, and as Robin Hood I had to have a sword fight with him. One day we were rehearsing this sword fight and for reasons best known to himself, the stage manager had given me a proper rapier that wasn't covered (no Health and Safety in those days!). Well, we were rehearsing this scene and I don't know which of us made a mistake, but somehow I pierced John in the forehead (thank God I just missed his eye). Of course, there was panic stations and he was rushed to hospital. Luckily it wasn't too bad—he just needed a couple of stitches and he forgave me!

I felt very bad about it though. One night, when there was thick fog, I was about to drive home from the theatre when John asked me for a lift as the buses weren't running. I could hardly say no, after nearly blinding him, so I drove to his place. He lived outside Manchester in Dukenfield on a little council estate with his family. I was quite surprised. I hadn't imagined such a flamboyant and well-spoken actor coming from such an ordinary background. His family were all really kind to me and I ended up staying the night, because by this time the fog had got really dense—one of those pea-soupers we used to have in those days—and I really couldn't find my way back to my parents' house. By the next morning it had lifted a bit and I managed to get home.

Later on, John became a well-known actor. He joined the Royal Shakespeare Company when Peter Hall was in charge and acted alongside Donald Sinden and Peggy Ashcroft, usually playing character parts. He made quite a few films too. He was in The Medusa Touch with Richard Burton. Many years later I went to London when he was in The Deep Blue Sea, a Terence Rattigan play, with Penelope Keith, which got very good reviews. There were pictures of him outside the theatre in the West End and I recognized him, though he'd gone bald by then and put on quite a bit of weight. He'd done very well for himself. I half thought about going in to see him, but I couldn't quite pluck up the courage. I suspected he might not have forgotten the incident with the rapier!

There's just one other thing I remember about Red Riding Hood. Towards the end of our run, Stanley Ross came to a performance and in the foyer bumped into the married couple who had been staying at the next apartment to ours when we were holidaying at The Roquebrun. Afterwards they all came round to my dressing room and he introduced me to them properly for the first time. Apparently, I wasn't quite such an embarrassment to him now that I was starring at his local theatre!

CHAPTER 8

t After Red Riding Hood finished, I went back to the club circuit for a while. A little Scottish girl called Lillian, who played the piano and sang, was doing the same clubs and we started doing a bit of a double act, which went down quite well.

Just before Easter 1960, Charlie Sharpe rang and asked me to go back to Le Couperon for the summer. This time he wanted me to do cabaret for the whole season. Of course, I was thrilled. I absolutely loved Jersey, but I didn't want to let Lillian down.

'The trouble is Charlie, I'm working with this girl and we've got a bit of a double act, 'I told him.

'Oh that's all right', Charlie said. 'Bring her with you and you can both work in the bar in the afternoons and do your act together in the evenings'. Lilian was happy with that and everything seemed set for a great summer.

But it didn't work out as well as I'd hoped. Lillian was a nice little girl but there was just one problem. Wherever Lillian went, mother came too. Her mother was a rather hard-bitten lady from the roughest part of Glasgow. She found herself a job in one of the cafes on the side of the pier at Rozel and when she'd finished work, Mother thought it was lovely to sit in the cocktail bar at Le Couperon in her moth-eaten fur coat drinking neat whisky while listening to her daughter singing.

Lilian herself also rubbed Charlie Sharpe up the wrong way. She used to wonder downstairs in the morning through the reception and gardens with her hair in her rollers. The pair of them just didn't fit in with the refined image Charlie was trying to create for his hotel. One day, he came to me and said I'm awfully sorry Joan, this isn't going to work out. We'd love you to stay, but I'm afraid Lilian and her mother have got to go!'

I had the embarrassing job of telling Lillian. She wasn't too pleased, but she found another job in one of the cabaret shows in a different part of Jersey and must have made a go of it, despite mother, because she went on to appear on television a few times. I was left to stay at Le Couperon singing little classical songs every night as the only entertainer and still had to work lots of hours in the bar as well. Eventually It all got to be too much for me, and I started looking round for alternative work.

One day, I heard that they wanted a singer at the Water 's Edge in Bouley Bay, which was about to re-open. In its heyday The Water's Edge had been a five-star hotel, but had got run down in recent years and a man called Leonard Matcham had bought it as a project. Mr Matcham had been an accountant to the stars and had obviously done very well out of that because he'd spent an awful lot of money doing the hotel up. When he had finished, it was the height of luxury. Mrs Matcham owned a mink farm and there was a lovely bar called the Mink Bar where all the stools were covered in mink tails. They even had a stuffed mink behind the bar advertising their 'mink' cocktails. It was all very fabulous. There was also a beautiful dining room, designed so that when the tide came in you could look out of the window and believe you were on board a ship.

Leonard Matcham had already booked Tibur Kunzler, a Hungarian gypsy violinist to perform for the season and he sent him to audition me in a hall near the Water's Edge. On Tibur's recommendation I was offered a job, so I then had to break the news to Charlie Sharpe.

'I'm sorry' I told him, 'But I didn't sign up to come back and work here in the bar every day, and I've been offered a job singing at the Water's Edge.

He knew the name at once. It had always been one of the best hotels on the island. 'Oooh,' he said 'Very top class!'

'It's going to be re-opening in a week or two so I'm afraid going to leave you.'

He smiled and shrugged 'Fair enough'.

So there were no hard feelings. In fact, Charlie Sharpe arranged to bring some visiting friends from Yorkshire to come over and see me appear in the first Gala performance on the opening night. It was set to be a really grand affair, with a special dinner and everyone in evening dress. The comedian Bob Monkhouse, who was already a very big name on TV, had been booked to be the star of the cabaret and I was the supporting singer. Before the show Leonard Matcham and Bob Monkhouse decided to go off to The Woodville at St Helier, which was another hotel that Leonard owned. I was sitting in the mink bar with my music when they swept past me on their way out. Bob Monkhouse waved to me "When we come back Joan, it's 'On with the show'", he promised.

To kill time while I sat in the bar waiting for them to return, I started chatting to some chap that I'd met in Leeds once, when I'd been playing there. He was a funny sort of fellow, with a bit of a speech impediment, who obviously wanted to impress me. He was sitting with another couple who he introduced as his brother (who he said was a film producer) and his brother's wife. It turned out that his wife used to be quite a well-known model called Violet Pretty and had once been the girlfriend of Carol Levis who ran talent shows, so she and I had quite an interesting chat over a couple of drinks. After an hour or so, when I was beginning to wonder if Bob Monkhouse and Leonard Matcham would ever return, the chap from Leeds turned to me" My brother's going back to Leeds tomorrow, but what if I order a hamper and you and I go on the beach and have a picnic?' He was a bit of a boring chap, but I said okay. I had nothing else to do.

Eventually, Bob Monkhouse and Leonard Matcham rushed back in through the bar and straight through to the ballroom. It turned out that Bob Monkhouse had been persuaded to do a bit of a spot at the Woodville and they had run late. A moment after they arrived, I heard the cabaret starting next door.

Nobody called for me, so I carried on sitting at the bar listening as Bob Monkhouse went on, did his stuff and finished to great applause. I thought I'd escaped, but suddenly Leonard Matcham walked into the bar, spotted me and said 'Oh my God I forgot all about you!'

'That's okay Mr Matcham. Don't worry' I said. But he grabbed my music from me and went into the ballroom, where he handed the musician the music and turned to the audience. 'There' s a little girl out there' he said pointing to me standing in the doorway. 'And she's brought her harp to the party and nobody's asked her to play' I was quite taken aback. What a bloody introduction!

Anyway I went on and gave my performance and everything went swimmingly well. It was a lovely audience.

When I came off, the press were there clicking their cameras and Bob Monkhouse was waiting. He threw his arms around me—I've got a photo of him somewhere kissing me! 'Darling. I wouldn't have done that to you for the world' he said. So in the end it was a great night.

My room at The Water's Edge wasn't yet ready for me, so after Bob Monkhouse left, I went back to Le Couperon. Charlie Sharpe and his Yorkshire guests had been sitting on the front row during the show and had then returned to Le Couperon. By the time I walked in to the bar they were all nice and merry. One of Charlie Sharpe's friends was Guy Reed, who was a very dashing ex RAF officer. Guy had made a fortune after the war when he left the RAF and started a frozen chicken firm called Buxted chickens.

They'd had a lovely evening at the opening night, seeing all the stars in the audience as well as listening to the show and when they saw me they invited me to join them. I sat in the cocktail bar drinking champagne and chatting with Guy Reed till dawn broke. Guy was a tall, strong, rather good looking man and I was quite taken with him. Eventually, as the party broke up, he turned to me and said, 'I've got an important meeting in Leeds tomorrow Joan, so I have to go back but will you have lunch with me before I leave?

I could have kicked myself. 'I'm sorry Guy, but I've fixed up to go for a picnic. This man I met today has ordered a hamper and he's picking me up at midday'.

'Oh for goodness sake, ditch him!' said Guy.

'Oh, I don't like to' I said. I had never stood anyone up in my life.

So Guy (later to be Sir Guy) went off in a huff, never to be seen again and I was stuck with this dreadful fellow on the beach. And that was that. Probably my only chance of getting together with a millionaire had gone!

The summer season at The Water's Edge was great fun. I sang both modern and old songs. Tibor Kunzler, who Len Matcham had booked after seeing him playing at Quaglino's, used to serenade people at the tables, and he also sang the odd duet with me. The pay was good, the audiences were good and my new accommodation, when I finally moved in, was five star, so I was happy.

Leonard Matcham was a good boss to work for, but quite intimidating until you got to know him. He was a big powerful man, very full of himself, as I suppose he was entitled to be. He had so much money, and of course he had this beautiful hotel (a few years later he was to be the subject of one of the Whicker's World programmes about the super-rich).

A lot of stars used to stay at the hotel and Leonard had this little trick of getting them to perform without paying them. When Anona Wynn was starring in the West End in Bless the Bride and came to stay for a break, he went over and put a microphone on her table and said 'Sing Winona' which brought the place down. He thought it was a great thing to do. Later, when Al Read the comedian came to stay with him he secretly put a microphone near his table. Al had become a very big radio star with his catchphrase 'You'll be lucky... I say. You'll be lucky'. So of course when he started ordering his meal, unaware that everything he said was being broadcast around the restaurant, everybody recognized his voice and turned around.

Al Read had his son staying with him who was a rather brash teenager—always trying out fake tan and wanting to go into town to see a bit of life. He thought the hotel was deadly dull.

One day, to my dismay, Len Matcham said to me 'Joan, take my car and drive this kid into town'. And I had to run him around in this Vauxhall belonging to the Matcham's. The minute we got out of sight of the hotel he started pestering me to drive it. 'Listen' I said 'you're not driving. You haven't got your license. And I'll be in trouble if you crash the car'. But he never stopped nagging at me all afternoon. Oh he was a pain. However, apparently Al read was an old friend of Len's and I had to do as I was told.

I had one rather strange encounter that summer. Although I didn't have to work as a barmaid any more, I occasionally used to take over the hotel switchboard for an hour or two to relieve the receptionist. One day, as I sat behind reception putting calls through who should walk n but Fred Pontin. I recognized him immediately, but he went sailing straight through without seeing me. Just at that moment the receptionist came back on duty. I pointed towards Fred's departing figure. 'I see we've got Fred Pontin booked in!'.

She looked puzzled 'Really? That's not who he said he was. He's booked in as Fred Smith'.

The next morning, I was on duty at the switchboard when the man came through to reception again. 'Oh good morning Mr Pontin' I said. 'How are you?' He looked startled 'Who are you?' he asked

'I'm Joan Booth. 'I said. 'You remember, I worked for you last year at Paignton?'

The penny dropped and he smiled 'What are you doing here Joan?'

'Well' I said, 'I'm singing tonight, but I'm working the switchboard this morning. I'm a Jill of all trades these days'.

'Oh, right.' he said. 'Will you have dinner with me after the cabaret?'

So after I did my act that night we went out to dinner and then we went dancing—I've still got a picture of me ballroom dancing with him.

As we danced, I quizzed him. 'What's the game then, calling yourself Fred Smith?'

He looked around as if to make sure nobody was listening before answering 'There's a holiday place here called Parkins in Plemont Bay, and it's for sale' he said 'I've got a man, Arthur Quantrill, who's put me in the picture that this could be bought and I'm going with him to have a look at it. Will you come with me?'

So I went along with these two and we went all round this holiday camp. Fred Pontin told Arthur Quantrill he was interested in it and between them they agreed to put in a bid.

I had dinner with Fred on a couple more occasions that week, then off he went, back to the mainland and I thought no more about it.

Several years later when I was married, some solicitors rang me up from London wanting to talk to me about our encounter in Jersey. Fred Pontin had gone on to buy Parkins and had turned it into a Pontin camp—and this man Quantrill was apparently claiming a big fee from him for negotiating the deal and had given my name to the solicitor as a witness to his role!

Another unexpected consequence of working at Le Couperon was that I found myself with a pet dog. As well as having a mink farm, Len Matcham's wife bred show poodles, and she had one little black toy poodle that wouldn't sell because it had an undershot jaw. Mrs Matcham said I could have it for £15 and I jumped at the offer. I called it Lenny, after her husband, who was a great big fellow, but always had a little poodle dangling on his arm.

Completely by chance, Lenny the poodle later became a part of my act while I was doing the clubs. I usually had a dressing room at the side of the stage and one day I can't have shut the dressing room door properly when I left it to go on stage. My party piece at the time was actually classical—Il Bacio, or 'The Kiss', by Luigi Arditi. The young Deanna Durbin had made it famous when she sang it in the film Three Smart Girls way back in the thirties. It was colora with lots of warbling. Anyway I was singing away when my little dog Lenny ran onto the stage. I picked him up—I couldn't think what else to do—and stuck him under my arm and carried on singing. Then suddenly as I sang, he started to howl. It brought the house down. So I thought 'Well this is good. Lenny could come in quite useful!' and after that, Lenny the poodle became a regular part of my act.

Towards the end of that summer season at The Water's Edge, Stanley Ross phoned me and said he was going on holiday at the end of September. Would I like to join him for two weeks in Majorca? It was a bit of a surprise. I hadn't actually broken off with Stanley, but I hadn't seen much of him since the year before. However, Majorca sounded appealing so I agreed.

After dropping Lenny off with my parents I flew with Stanley from Manchester to Magaluf, which nowadays is like Blackpool, but in those days, was quite exclusive. For a long time, it only had one big hotel called the Atlantic in the middle of this lovely bay with a little island about a mile or so out. They'd just started building a new hotel on the side called the Flamboyan which Stanley had booked us into.

it was a very nice hotel with a cocktail bar and swimming pool and I spent my time doing yet more sunbathing and swimming. There was an American GI staying at the hotel with his French girlfriend. I think Stanley was quite shocked by the girlfriend, who used to go out topless on a pedalo around the bay. This GI took quite a shine to me and I didn't exactly discourage him. In those days I was an awful flirt I'm afraid, and the novelty of Stanley was beginning to wear off. He had lots of irritating little habits, not least of which was breaking wind very loudly in public, which he seemed to find terribly funny.

I quickly made friends among the other hotel guests and one night, a gang of us, including the GI, went skinny dipping. Poor Stanley Ross didn't swim. He'd had polio as a child and he had rather funny little legs. So he stayed on the shore as we all ran naked across the beach in the moonlight and dived into the sea. There were patches of long weeds under the water and as I was swimming through them I could feel them flowing around against my legs. All of a sudden, something wrapped around my foot. It really hurt and I went 'Eeeow!!!'

Everybody was laughing and screaming so much that nobody took much notice of me. Eventually I managed to kick my foot free and swam back to the beach where Stanley was standing with a big towel to put around me. To my horror, when I lifted up my foot you could see the marks of a squid's tentacles all around my foot and ankle. it must have been a big one. And it had grabbed me! I turned to the others and said 'Now do you believe me?'. It caused great consternation among the rest of the group.

One day, more bored than ever with Stanley's company, I decided to swim out to the island in the bay. I wasn't a fancy swimmer, but because I'd swum every day in Jersey, I could do the breast stroke forever (probably all my singing and breath control helped too). I had a snorkel, so I was able to take my time and look down in the water at all these lovely coloured fish as I swam. Once I got to the island, I hauled myself out, and had a little sunbathe. I was completely unaware that back on the beach my gang of new friends were doing a little fandango, saying 'Where's she gone? She was swimming out there...' Of course, when they saw me swimming back they all rushed down and as I walked out of the water, Stanley said crossly 'What on earth did you think you were doing?'

I couldn't understand why he was making such a fuss. 'But I wasn't in any trouble' I said. 'It was calm water. I just took my time and swam out and swam back'.

'Do you know how far out it was?' he said. I said I thought about a mile or two. "But you've been out there for hours!" he exclaimed. I'd been gone a long time because I'd been there and back, but I wasn't in any danger.

Unlike Stanley, all the others in our group thought it was wonderful. The next day some of the women said 'Will you come out swimming with us? Will you take us out to the island?' I said 'Yes, I'll go with you again, but if you get into trouble, don't expect me to save you! I'm not a life saver. I can only do the breast stroke!' So I set off again with these women, me plodding on with my breast stroke and this German lady doing the crawl very elegantly and we had just got to the entrance to the bay when the German lady shrieked 'Oh I've got cramp' and the others all panicked. All around me, people were splashing wildly and saying 'Help, we can't go any further', so I had to turn around and take them all back. The GI was lying on the beach watching us and I noticed he seemed rather impressed!

A day or two later I was swimming out in the bay again when he joined me and we swam out to where the bay curves around. Suddenly he hauled me towards him and started kissing me, saying he wanted to see more of me and could he write to me. I said 'But you've got this classy French dame here!'

'Oh no" he said 'she's just a passing fancy'. And he did write to me. He was posted out to Lagos or somewhere but I got a few letters from him when I got back to England.

Not surprisingly, Stanley soon cottoned on that this man was paying me a lot of attention and I was enjoying it, so he wasn't too pleased about that. He'd bought me a rather expensive present—a silk Hermes scarf—and a few days later, when we were packing up to go back, I noticed the scarf was missing. I suspected he'd whipped it back!

We didn't have much to say to each other on the journey back to England. He had left his car at Manchester airport and he drove me home in silence. When we finally arrived back at the door of my parents' house and I got out of his car, he handed me a big coloured photo of myself which he'd asked me for months before.

"Here, you can have this back 'he said. 'You're obviously no longer interested in me, and anyway I've found another girlfriend'.

'Oh, did she like the scarf?" I asked

He glared at me 'Yes as a matter of fact, she did.' Then he drove off to his home in Stockport and that was the last I ever saw of Stanley!

CHAPTER 9

The whole time I was in Jersey that summer Frank had been telephoning me regularly. Frank was one of a family of seven boys, nearly all of whom had ended up as bar tenders. Funnily enough, three of them had actually been at Jersey while I was there. Danny worked at the Dolphin in Goreye and had come over to meet me while I was at Le Couperon. The two other brothers, Patrick and John were both working at The Moorings, which was also in Goreye.

Frank though, was still working at the Duke of Edinburgh in Oldham. After I returned from Majorca, I rang the hotel to have a chat to him.

The person who answered the phone said 'Oh, I'm afraid I can't get him for you. He's in hospital'.

My heart missed a beat. Although I'd grown very fond of Frank in the two years since I'd first met him, I was surprised by how worried I felt.

'Oh dear, what's the matter with him?' I asked. The person on the phone was a bit vague, so I jumped into my car the very same day and drove over to Ashton to visit him in hospital.

I found Frank propped up in bed looking dreadful. He was very pale and his breathing was wheezy as he explained what had happened. I already knew that the Whittakers, the couple who managed the Duke of Edinburgh, were real slave drivers. Recently, Frank had told me he'd had enough of them and had applied for another job. They had a little boy and although Frank was in the cocktail bar till two or three in the morning, he was expected to get up around seven and take this child to school. One day, as he'd got out of bed he'd felt an awful pain in the side of his chest. He went to the doctor and saw a locum, who didn't think it was serious 'You've probably strained a muscle in the cellar, lifting barrels or something' he told Frank.

So Frank carried on working until one morning, a few days later, he woke up feeling so ill he couldn't get out of bed to take this child to school. His pyjamas were wringing wet through. The hotel managers sent for a doctor, who immediately rushed him into hospital. It turned out he had pleurisy and was told he would have to stay in hospital for weeks because there was fluid on his lungs. He had always been quite a heavy smoker, but the doctors told him he must never smoke again.

After a while they sent him to Southport to recuperate, but they wouldn't let him out till he'd got rid of a shadow which the pleurisy had left on his lungs. (He was always susceptible to pleurisy after that and used to get it at odd times through the rest of his life). While he was in Southport he decided he was going to accept a job which he'd recently been offered at a pub in Mansfield.

I felt really sorry for Frank. Up until now I hadn't really taken him seriously, but I was beginning to realise that I cared about him more than I wanted to admit. He wasn't bad looking, but it was his personality I'd fallen for. He was so funny. As I'd slowly got to know him, I'd realised what a character he was. He was such a young man, four years younger than me, and very naïve when I first met him. In the three years since then though, he had matured and developed and I had got to like him more and more.

My grandmother still lived in her cottage in Mellor, high up in the Peak district. The area had been noted as a good place to recuperate since the olden days. People suffering from TB used to go up there because it was good for their lungs. So I said to Frank 'Come up to my grandmother's. It'll do you good'. I drove him up to Mellor and we stayed with my grandmother for nearly a week. Grandma got on very well with Frank. She was quite a character herself and I think she recognized a kindred spirit. We went for lots of walks and drives out into the countryside. Towards the end of our stay, Frank plucked up his courage and proposed to me for the first time.

We had been enjoying each other's company, but even so, I was completely taken aback. I tried to put him off as gently as I could. 'Well we don't really know each other that well, Frank' I said. 'Let's find out a bit more before we make any decisions.'

Poor Frank, He was young and innocent and he was a virgin. But when he proposed, I decided it was time put a stop to that! On his way to go back to work at Mansfield we booked into the Cavendish hotel near Baslow, where we spent the night together and I taught him a few things that he didn't know! He was really hooked then, and was desperately keen for us to get engaged. But much as I liked him, I didn't want to get married. I was still ambitious and I didn't feel ready to give up my career and settle down. I promised Frank only that I would think about it.

.

Before I'd set off for Majorca Len Matcham had asked me to return at Christmas and New Year to do cabaret in the Woodville in St Helier which, unlike the Water's Edge, he used to keep going through the winter. I went back for Christmas to the Woodville taking my little dog Lenny with me. and when I arrived at the hotel reception Len was all smiles and greeted me like an old friend. 'Oh come into the dining room' he said. He led me to a table and sat me down and then he played his old party trick on me. He called for a microphone and put it on the table. 'Now' he said 'when I switch it on, start singing'

Well, none of the other diners knew me. What a stupid thing to do! I just didn't know how to react. Then, as I was wondering what to do I hesitantly touched the microphone and suddenly it went bang and sparks started flying—it was live! So that scotched that idea. And was I grateful!

I discovered that since he had booked me, Len had also booked the singer Matt Munro for Christmas. It was a lucky coup for him as Matt Munro had just had a very big hit with a song called Portrait of My Love and his career was about to take off.

Matt was there with his wife Micki. He did the pop stuff, while I did songs from the shows. The whole experience was very nice. Every night, after the show we all used to meet Leonard Matcham in the bar. Matt was very good at telling jokes, which amused Matcham. So we'd all have a drink together and I'd go off to bed.

After the Christmas cabaret finished, Len asked. 'Will you come back to the Water's Edge at Easter and do the summer season Joan? I said 'Yes I'd love to'. I had intended to return to Jersey whatever happened, but another season at the Water's Edge was ideal because I'd really enjoyed my time there. I decided to be cheeky and ask if I could bring my sister Anne with me. Anne had been having love problems. She'd been working as a typist for a solicitor who she'd fallen for in a big way. But in my opinion it was going nowhere. He came from quite a well-to-do family—who were all big wheels at the local golf club. He still lived at home and I didn't believe Anne's boyfriend was ever going to be brave enough to tell his middle class parents that he was dating the office typist.

'Oh forget about him Anne', I'd told her. 'Come to Jersey with me and have a good time'. She'd agreed and when I told him, Leonard Matcham said he's find work for her in reception.

I put the booking in my diary. On the two previous occasions I'd worked for him I'd never had any written contract with Len Matcham. We'd just agreed what I'd do and everything had fallen into place. So I wasn't worried that he didn't ask me to sign any paperwork. But this time, relying on word of mouth was to prove a big mistake.

I didn't bother ringing beforehand, as it was only three months since we'd arranged it, and just before Easter, I arrived with Anne and my little poodle Lenny at The Water's Edge. This time Leonard Matcham wasn't there to greet me. We were shown to a room and I had just started to unpack when the head waiter appeared. He had been given the dirty job of telling us that our services were no longer required. It seemed Leonard Matcham had seen a male pianist entertainer at some restaurant in London, booked him there and then and hadn't had the guts to let me know.

I was a bit put out, to say the least. But there was no point in arguing. After a spot of quick thinking, I decided to go to Parkinson's in Piemont Bay where I knew some of the staff and offered to sing for my supper there. They booked us in and let us stay there for a night in return for me singing a few songs in the bar.

'Right Anne', I said the next day. 'I'd better get cracking'.

So off I went and set off round around the Jersey hotels looking for work. By the end of the week I had found myself jobs all over the place—an hour's spot here; another hour there.

We found a room to rent in a farmhouse. We could do our washing there but had to hang it out on the bushes to dry. It was a bit off the beaten track, so I hired a big old Riley to get us about. It was built like a tank and for the rest of the summer I used it to drive myself in it between two or three different places every night.

My first spot was usually cabaret at the L'Horizon hotel in St Brelades Bay where they had a string quartet which played light classical music in the Albert Sandler style. I would wear an evening dress for that show and sing classical songs and arias. All very prim and proper. Underneath though, I would be wearing tights and a leotard, and after I'd done my bit at the L'Horizon, I'd leap into the car, whip off my skirt, straighten my tights, and go on to the Chateau Plaisir on the St Ouen's Road where people used to arrive by the coachload for a boozy night with live entertainment.

There, I'd do cabaret stuff around the tables and sit on men's knees and sing while a photographer took pictures which he'd sell to them afterwards. I'd be singing 'I'm in the mood for love' to them and flirting, while this photographer snapped away. A photo of me must have gone home to a lot of places that summer so men could show it to their friends and brag 'Look what I caught on holiday!'

By way of payment for my services the photographer would take Anne and me out for a slap up meal afterwards, so we were all happy.

I also got a regular spot at the very elegant Hotel de France in St Helier where Elaine Del Mar, who was a good coloured soul singer was also booked. She would do a spot one night and I'd do one the next. Elaine's father, Leslie 'Jiver' Hutchinson was a jazz trumpeter and was a resident entertainer at another hotel in Jersey that year.

Yet another of my regular bookings in St Helier was at the Hotel Revere which was a very good St Helier restaurant. By the end of the summer I had got myself spots all around the island and was making myself a packet doing two or three spots a night. I found Anne a typing job in the office of a firm who ran coaches round the island. She used to come with me in the evenings and she started going out with a chap from one of the local bands. We had a great time—it was good fun.

All the time we were there, Ann's solicitor boyfriend was writing to her. I used to dictate her letters back to him. I said 'Let's wind him up a bit. We'll get him going, Don't say you're missing him whatever you do'. So her letters told him what a good time she was having, and that she was seeing this chap in the band, and never carried a hint that she was crying into her pillow over him every night (which she was). It worked. When we got back he proposed and it wasn't too long before she married him!

While I'd been in Jersey Frank had decided that the job in Mansfield didn't suit him after all and had found another one in Morecombe at a hotel on the front. I visited him there as soon as `I arrived home. My position regarding marriage hadn't changed, but it was good to see him again.

I was really missing stage work and tried to find some that Autumn. But it proved to be impossible. Recently all the theatres had moved away from shows with Ivor Novello music and operettas like The Merry Widow and Lilac Time, and were staging modern musicals like Annie get your Gun and The Pajama Game with a lot of dancing. That meant they now wanted dancers who could sing rather than 'singer' singers…

As a result, I once again found myself working the Northern clubs. In many ways it was quite a funny period. I was still very brown after all my sunbathing in Jersey and Majorca and in the early sixties in the little mining villages of Yorkshire they'd never seen people with tans before, so to them I suppose I looked quite exotic. I certainly attracted quite a lot of male attention, culminating in that flight to Le Touquet in Fred's little plane!

For the most of the following year I continued to tour the club circuit. I also continued to see quite a lot of Frank, who had moved jobs yet again. This time he was doing what he was best at, making and serving cocktails, at a brand new venture called the Square and Compass in Harrogate. This was a very classy inn, owned by the Gale Lister company, which in its first few months had taken off as one of the top restaurants in the area. All the horse-racing people used to go there, which was great for Frank, because following the horses was of his passions. He was quite adept at taking advantage of inside knowledge and he took a lot of money off the bookies that year.

One of Frank's regular customers was a big jeweller called Mr Dyson who had a shop on the Headrow in Leeds. When Frank told him that he was 'almost' engaged, Mr Dyson had apparently told him that he had the perfect ring for me. A lovely old-fashioned one with beautiful diamonds. '

'There's just one problem 'said Frank 'She hasn't said yes, yet'.

'Never mind' said Mr Dyson. 'I'll put it in the safe for you and you can tell me when you want it'. And that was how it was left.

Towards the end of 1962 I was beginning to get really fed up of doing the clubs. It was quite lonely work and I much preferred the theatre with all its behind the scenes camaraderie. In October, Frank Mulling's wife came to my rescue and booked me to do a pantomime in Llandudno. It was rather a strange set-up. The pantomime in question was Cinderella and it was being funded and organised by some woman who had a little café in Conway, but had always dreamed of putting on a pantomime. Somehow she had convinced the theatrical agents that it was a legitimate set-up and several good artists had been booked.

So from all over the country we converged on this place in Conway. Unfortunately, everyone had been misled. The whole set-up was totally unprofessional. The café owner was simply star-struck. She wined and dined us nearly every night but we just weren't getting down to rehearsals and the nitty gritty. After a few days we started raising our eyebrows and looking at each other, thinking this is a bit of a funny going on. The woman had ordered lots of lovely costumes and props but after the first week's rehearsals we still hadn't been given a proper producer or director. And we were supposed to open two weeks before Christmas. There were some good people in the show who were being absolutely wasted. It was just chaos.

The climax came on payday at the end of our opening week when it turned out the woman couldn't afford to pay us. Since we were all members of Equity, the actors Union, they were brought in to sort it out and we were paid by them, but not surprisingly, the whole thing folded.

When I came home I rang Frank and I told him I was back at my parents and out of a job.

He said 'But I thought you were principal boy?'

'I was, but it's all over…' I replied.

'Well', said Frank after I'd explained. 'Don't despair. There just might be a job for you here!' It turned out my phone call was perfectly timed. Frank told me that the Square and Compass had booked Fred Emney to do cabaret that Christmas. Fred was a big fat man who played the piano and told funny stories in a posh English accent. He was quite a big star, not only on television, but also in films—he'd recently acted in The Italian Job. He'd been booked to entertain all the best people in Yorkshire as they wined and dined at the Square and Compass in the lead up to Christmas. But Fred Emney's opening night had been a disaster. He'd walked onstage, sat at his piano, did a little bit of a party piece, told a little bit of a story and then turned to the audience and said "Well. I'll be in the bar if you'd like to buy me a drink" before getting up and staggering off. Of course, Yorkshire people weren't standing for that. They were all up in arms, complaining 'We haven't paid this much just to see that'. Eventually, the management had to go to Frank Emney's hotel and tell him he couldn't get away with that and pay him off.

'So do you think you could come to the Square and Compass this weekend?' Frank asked. 'They're desperate for a replacement cabaret act. I'll ask them if they'd like you to come and sing for them.'

A few moments later the phone rang again and Frank said. You're booked!'

The pub managers also wanted to find a comedian to replace Fred Emney, so I rang a chap I'd recently worked with in the clubs who had started an agency. I asked him if he knew a good comedian with a sophisticated sense of humour and he said. 'Yes, I have just the man. He's a bit of a Bob Monkhouse type and he just happens to be free'.

The next day, the comedian and I arrived in Harrogate to save the day.

I had taken Lenny with me, and before the first show I said to Frank. 'I'm going to go on in tights and leotard and I'll announce that I'm going to introduce them to my boyfriend. When I say that, you release Lenny and he'll come flying into my arms and I'll sit him up beside me and I'll sing The Trish Trash Polka!'

And that's exactly what I did. The Square and Compass had a very good resident pianist who accompanied me—and as soon as I hit the high notes Lenny would join in, his mouth forming a little '0' and soon the diners were rolling in the aisles. It was so funny. The whole cabaret was a great success. The comedian went down a bomb and I went down a bomb.

For the next ten days I did three spots a night and my mate the comedian did three spots so they got a lot better value than with Fred Emney!

During that time, I got to know some of Frank's new colleagues. Two of them in particular were to become great friends: Peter Fothergill, who was the sommelier wine waiter and his wife Nancy, who was a silver service waitress. When we'd finished our last show at the Square and Compass we all went out for the evening to celebrate at The Owl at Selby, which in those days was a club. Denny Dennis a retired crooner who had once been a big star, was doing cabaret there and we had a wonderful time dancing and letting our hair down.

I don't know if it was the wine or the adrenaline from my recent performance but something that night made me finally come to my senses. I realised I'd had enough of the clubs. My career wasn't going anywhere now. Yes, I thought, I've had a good run. It's been a lot of fun, but maybe it's time I packed it in.

Full of bubbles and allowing myself no time for second thoughts, I turned to the lovely Irishman on my left and announced 'All right Frank I'll marry you!'.

And so a new chapter of my life began…

HYDE AMATEUR
LIGHT OPERA
COMPANY

Mr.
CINDERS

OCTOBER
13th-18th 1947

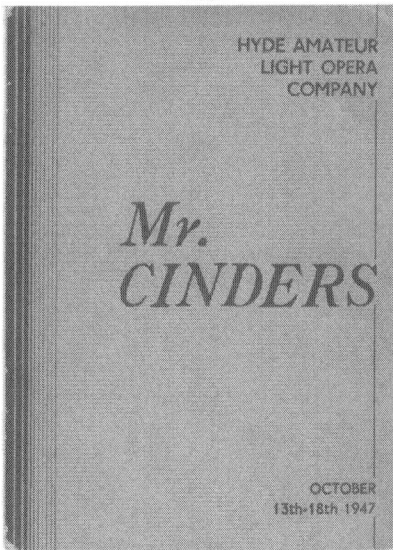

Souvenirs of my first stage performances as a schoolgirl.

My first principal boy role—as Dandini in Cinderella.

As Robin Hood in Red Riding Hood with John Normington

Chatting up the punters in Jersey's Chateau Plaisir Hotel!

My first workplace in Jersey-Le Couperon at Rozel.

Dressed to kill and ready for cabaret!

An early publicity photograph with my hair up.

And one with my hair down! (front of house publicity poster)

With Frank at another Bar Tenders Guild dinner at Harrogate.

I finally said 'Yes!" My wedding to Frank in October 1963

ABOUT THE AUTHOR

Joan Campbell lives in Macclesfield, Cheshire. In 1963, after 15 years as a professional singer, she retired from the stage and became a pub landlady. When her husband, Frank, died in 2004 she started writing her memoirs. Joan is currently working on a second volume, recounting anecdotes from her 32 years behind the bar. She continues to enjoy singing, horse-racing and travel. Joan has one son, Michael, who works in advertising.

Printed in Great Britain
by Amazon